WALKING THROUGH WINTER

Katherine Gantlett

instant
apostle

First published in Great Britain in 2021

Instant Apostle
104 The Drive
Rickmansworth
Herts
WD3 4DU

Every effort has been made to seek permission to use copyright material reproduced in this book. The publisher apologises for those cases where permission might not have been sought and, if notified, will formally seek permission at the earliest opportunity.

The views and opinions expressed in this work are those of the author and do not necessarily reflect the views and opinions of the publisher.

British Library Cataloguing-in-Publication Data

A catalogue record for this book is available from the British Library.

This book and all other Instant Apostle books are available from Instant Apostle:

Website: www.instantapostle.com

Email: info@instantapostle.com

ISBN 978-1-912726-41-7

Printed in Great Britain.

For all my children
With love
Mummy

Contents

Acknowledgements

They say it takes a village to raise a child; well, it's taken a whole town-full of people to raise this book!

To my husband and my 'brick' Jon, you are the very best of men. Thank you for your love, loyalty and laughter – particularly in the depths of winter. And thank you for your encouragement and patience, without which this book would not have come to be. I love you more than my words can ever express.

To my gorgeous boy, Charlie. Thank you for all the joy and laughter you bring into my life. You truly are a 'bringer of light'.

Mum and Dad – thank you for your love, encouragement and wisdom along the way. I love you both very much.

To our families, thank you for your love and support which kept us warm in the depths of winter.

To my soul friends, Catherine, Jo S, Ali, Liesel, Anne and Sarah. Thank you for your love, wisdom and prayer-full commitment to me. Thank you for having the faith to carry me to Jesus when I had none. Thank you to Jo and Catherine for reading the first draft of this manuscript, and for your encouragement to persevere to see this story on paper.

To my *anam cara*, Kayla, I am deeply grateful to you for walking alongside me on my journey towards the heart of God.

To Sam, thank you for your beautiful artwork that graces the cover of this book and for being the listener to God and others that you are.

To Ness, thank you for encouraging me to study with WTC, for going without food on a Thursday for so long and for your collection of white feathers. You truly have been the lady that God placed in my life for 'such a time as this'.

Thank you to the wonderful team of midwives at the John Radcliffe Hospital who cared for me and Jon during Libby's birth and in the days afterwards. I am also so grateful for the dedication and commitment to anyone affected by the death of a baby shown by the team at Sands.

Thank you to Kay for the beautiful flowers placed with love on our doorstep each week through the depths of our winter.

To Jane, a fellow member of my tribe. Thank you for all the cups of tea and for encouraging me to write my 'Letters to Libby', from which the idea for this book was conceived. I know our little girls are proud of us.

To my amazing family and friends who literally walked alongside Jon and me as we climbed Kilimanjaro. Thank you for going far more than the extra mile with us.

I am deeply grateful to have been part of the WTC community as I walked through winter. Thank you to Lucy, Matt, Brad, Crispin and all the WTC staff and my fellow students, particularly the community at the Hampshire Hub. Thank you for holding me and loving me through it all.

To my wonderful community of friends whose love warmed us through the bleakest parts of winter. There are too many of you to name but I hope you know who you are and know that I love you.

To Felix, thank you for rescuing my summer this year when the coronavirus pandemic hit and for entertaining Charlie so well while I locked myself away in the study to write. His bike-riding tricks and train track building abilities are all thanks to you!

Thank you to the 'Chariots of Fire' ladies for all the free therapy sessions as we ran this year. I am looking forward to more runs with you all.

Thank you to Jo for putting my body back together after my many runs or when I have spent too long sitting writing.

I owe a huge debt of gratitude to my friend and copy editor Nicki Copeland. Thank you for having the courage to call this book into being all those years ago. Thank you for being my 'midwife', working alongside me and encouraging me to bring this project to fruition.

Thank you to all at Instant Apostle for working with me to realise this dream.

Finally, thank you, precious three, Father, Son and Holy Spirit, for Your promise that You are with us always. Thank You for Your love, faithfulness, guidance, companionship, comfort and counsel, all of which empowered me to walk on through winter.

Foreword

by Matt Lynch, Assistant Professor of Old
Testament, Regent College, Vancouver

In his *Lament for a Son*, Nicholas Wolterstorff writes of resisting
the urge to act strong when faced with loss. 'Wounds are ugly,'
he acknowledges, but hastens to add this question, 'But must
they always be swathed?' There's enormous pressure on those
of us who are Christians to *show that we're different from the world,
to be a witness, to display the joy of the LORD*. These lofty aims often
lead us to hide our wounds, our pain, and our sorrow.
Everything from the songs we sing to the leaders we elevate can
seem geared toward pain avoidance. In the process, our wounds
fester and we suffer in silence. It doesn't have to be this way.
Wolterstorff continues with bold resolve, 'I shall look at the
world through tears. Perhaps I shall see things that dry-eyed I
could not see.'

Katherine has chosen to see the world through tears. *Walking
Through Winter* brings us through her story of suffering and
lament (and, eventually, hope) that accompanied the loss of her
daughter Libby and five miscarriages. Her tears don't distort
reality. They bring it into sharp focus.

Over the years, I've had the privilege of watching Katherine
fight for a deeper faith, even as she and Jon journeyed in and
through the anguish and emptiness of loss. I have learned
immensely from her willingness to remain open toward God
and others during the acute crisis and during the long war of

attrition on her soul. By watching her walk through winter, I've learned more about what conformity to Christ looks like, and what it means to experience the fellowship with Christ that comes only through participating in his sufferings (Phil 3:10).

Katherine writes that Christians don't need more maps and guidebooks to show 'how to' puzzle their way through suffering. They need reliable guides. Katherine is a reliable guide who knows how to navigate the frozen terrain of loss, but also knows that there are many routes through. *Walking Through Winter* gives us an eye-opening and honest look at her particular experiences, but in a way that will translate into the experiences of others.

Katherine is a reliable guide because she grounds her reflections in the rich soil of Scripture and theology. To survive the wilds of winter, you need that first-hand knowledge of food sources, how to find shelter, and how to read weather patterns and signs. That knowledge doesn't come through guesswork alone. *Walking Through Winter* reflects Katherine's own experiences, to be sure, but also the wisdom of the ages that she learned through years of theological study. It may seem strange to study theology while experiencing a personal crisis, as she did. But I wish more people would, because Scripture and the Christian tradition have so much to offer us today.

Christians need the wisdom of winter. In his book *A Glorious Dark*, A J Swoboda talks about the need for a fully formed Friday–Saturday–Sunday faith. Good Friday Christianity acknowledges the grief and loss. Holy Saturday embraces the doubts. And Resurrection Sunday leaps forth in praise. Katherine's book is a plea for Christians to develop a Four Seasons faith. Its focus is winter, because it's the season that most Christians who seek continuous 'growth' ignore. But her sights are on the development of a mature faith that knows how to meet God in all seasons, because we – and those we love – will go through them again. It's winter, but signs of spring are there.

The insights in this book are cold-forged in Katherine's own winter of suffering, and so it's both deep and practical. As you journey through this book, and consider your own winter, I pray that Katherine's words will minister to you as they have to so many of us.

Part 1

Setting out

Where are we going?

Walk with me and work with me – watch how I do it.
Matthew 11:29 (*The Message*)

The Quaker writer and retreat leader Parker Palmer writes that a calling is 'something you can't not do'.[1] This is how writing this book has felt. It has taken me more than seven years to get our story down on paper. In that time, there have been many occasions when I have tried to let this project go. Partly because it has felt like such a battle; the words have not always flowed and, in writing our story, I have had to relive all we walked through in our winter season of catastrophic loss. But every time I have tried to let it go it wouldn't leave me alone.

When something is hard, it can be a struggle to discern why this is. Have we picked up something that God never intended us to carry? Or is this a battle we need to persevere through? Is there something precious in the work that will lead to transformation either for ourselves or for others, or both? During one of my times of really wanting to be released from this project, I was out walking, asking God this exact question. I felt Him say the following to me: 'Think about the times when you let go of something that I did not intend for you to carry, or where the season was over and you needed to release the fruit

---

[1] Parker J Palmer, *Let Your Life Speak: Listening for the Voice of Vocation* (Jossey Bass, 2000), p25.

and move on. How did this feel? Now think about how you feel about putting this book project down.' As I reflected on this, I realised that in the times when I have released things that I needed to let go of, there was always a sense of freedom and liberation that came from putting it down. However, this is never how I have felt about letting this writing project go. This project is challenging and sacrificial. But it is something that I can't not do.

I am not one for seeing a spiritual battle under every stone. Sometimes our wrestle is with the spiritual forces lined up against us, but at other times our wrestle is with God. In his book *Sacred Fire*, Roman Catholic priest Ronald Rolheiser retells the beautiful story of a young man asking an old monk whether he still wrestles with the devil. His response? 'Not any longer … I wrestle with God.'[2]

When I think about wrestling with God, I find myself drawn to the story of Jacob's wrestle with Him (Genesis 32:22-32). Interestingly, Jacob's wrestle took place at night, and it released a new identity in him. For me, the similarities are striking: my wrestle took place through the darkness of catastrophic loss, but through it God has released blessing and, just as He gave a new name to Jacob, He has released a new identity in me.

Walking on water

I think I have also struggled to write this book because I feel like I am taking a considerable risk. Through its pages I am 'baring my soul' – the good, the bad and the ugly! I also feel slightly presumptuous about suggesting ways to help others walking a similar path; I don't feel like an expert at all.

---

[2] Ronald Rolheiser, *Sacred Fire: A Vision for a Deeper Human and Christian Maturity* (Image, New York, 2014), p4.

One of my favourite authors is Brené Brown, who writes about 'wholehearted living'.[3] The original meaning of the word 'courage' comes from the Latin word for heart – *cor*. Brown writes, 'In one of its earliest forms, the word *courage* meant "to speak one's mind by telling all one's heart".'[4] We have reduced courage to bravery in the face of battles, but it is so much more than this. Courageous people are those who are willing to be vulnerable – to tell all of their hearts. Vulnerability is what gives us the ability to take down the mask that we all wear, the cover that says, 'I'm good; I have life sorted,' and instead relate to others in a far more authentic way. This struck a chord with me, and since reading some of Brené's work, I am trying to live a more 'wholehearted life'.

Writing this book is part of that commitment; this is me trying to live wholeheartedly. I hope you'll find here an authentic account of my journey through a winter season. I have wanted to be honest about the darkness of this season in terms of the pain, heartbreak and confusion, as well as sharing how I found the light of love, hope, purpose and, dare I say it, joy amid the darkness. I want to share the reality of my winter journey in the hope that those reading this might know that they are not alone, that there are others out there who 'get it'.

This is scary, and it's a risk, but it's also exciting. As a Christian, I believe that is what faith in Jesus is all about – that weird mix of being scared by the risk you are taking but also excited to see what God will do. Taking risks is what God has always called His people to do.

One of my favourite Gospel stories is when Peter walks on water with Jesus (Matthew 14:22-32). Yes, he sank, but Jesus

---

[3] For a great introduction to Brené Brown's work, see her TED talk entitled 'The Power of Vulnerability',
https://www.ted.com/talks/brene_brown_the_power_of_vulnerability (accessed 5th November 2020).
[4] Brené Brown, *I Thought It Was Just Me (But It Isn't): Making the Journey from 'What Will People Think?' to 'I Am Enough'* (Avery, New York, 2008), p xxiii.

rescued him, and, crucially, for the rest of his life he knew what it was like to walk on water, unlike the rest of the disciples who stayed in the boat. Stepping out of my boat and giving this a go feels like a risk. But I'd rather know how this turns out than live with a 'what if?' I also trust Jesus that He'll not let me drown.

Why winter?

Why have I chosen the metaphor of the seasons? Firstly, because I am married to a farmer. This means our lives are inextricably linked with the seasons of nature. The rhythm of our lives changes with the seasons as Jon's work varies according to the seasons. Our lifestyle is unusual in our culture. We are a society that has become divorced from the natural world in so many ways. Most of us work inside and have jobs that have no link to nature's seasons, and we buy our food in supermarkets where it doesn't matter what time of year it is – we can always buy strawberries!

Secondly, I've chosen a metaphor from nature because I believe the natural world has a lot to teach us about how to live well. As Galileo said, God has written two books: the Book of Scripture – the Bible – and the Book of Nature, and they communicate complementary truths.[5] I find being out in nature restorative; it is a place where I feel more connected with my soul and hence with God. The natural world is a 'thin place', somewhere I go to meet with God, and where He regularly communicates His truth to me through my surroundings.

In addition, seasons of loss in our lives share many similarities with the natural season of winter. They can be pretty bleak, cold and dark. Often, they are times in life where the abundance and fruitfulness of other seasons feel like a distant memory. Just like a deciduous tree is stripped back to bare

---

[5] Galileo, Letter to the Grand Duchess Christina of Tuscany (1615), verses 272-279.

branches, we can feel like our lives have been stripped right back too.

However, winter is not all bad. Consider the beauty of a clear, bright, frosty morning, or the silence that descends with the falling snow, or the joy of a snowball fight. There is a real beauty to be found in the natural world during winter. Moreover, this season of dormancy, of being stripped back, lays the foundation for the new life that bursts forth each spring.

Winter is also a season of retreat, of cosying up inside, reading great books, watching favourite films, or sharing good food with friends and family. This is a practice the Danes call *hygge*, which is essentially the art of creating intimacy. Happiness researcher Meik Wiking writes:

> Hygge is about an atmosphere and an experience, rather than about things. It is about being with the people we love. A feeling of home. A feeling that we are safe, that we are shielded from the world and allow ourselves to let our guard down.[6]

Danish winters are known to be among the longest, coldest and darkest in the world. However, despite this, in global happiness polls, Denmark consistently ranks in the top ten.[7] Could one of the reasons for this be that Danes have learnt how to embrace winter through the practice of *hygge?*

---

[6] Meik Wiking, *The Little Book of Hygge: The Danish Way to Live Well* (Penguin Life, UK, 2016), p6.
[7] Frank Martela, Bent Greve, Bo Rothstein and Juho Saari, 'The Nordic Exceptionalism: What Explains Why the Nordic Countries are Constantly Among the Happiest in the World', in 'The World Happiness Report 2020', https://worldhappiness.report/ (accessed 5th November 2020).

Wisdom walks

After our daughter Libby died, a very dear friend gave me a card with a poem written by Andy Raine, entitled 'Walking with Grief'. This poem beautifully articulates the truth that, much as we might want to, we can't hurry our way through grief.[8]

Walking in nature in winter is much the same. I love walking up on the Uffington White Horse, which is close to where we live. In the summer I find I can stride out along the ancient Ridgeway footpath that tracks across White Horse Hill. However, in the wintertime, my pace is slower; I have to be much more cautious, watching out for patches of ice on frosty mornings, or I simply find myself slowed down by all the mud! Frustrating as it is to slacken my pace, when I do, something extraordinary happens: I am far more present to my surroundings. I notice details that I miss as I stride through the same place in summer. More than this, with the stripping back that comes with winter, things that were hidden behind dense foliage are now revealed. Through the bare branches I can see more and further than I could in summer.

What's true in nature is true in our lives too. If we allow ourselves to walk slowly with grief, we can be more fully present to God, ourselves and others on our journey. I also believe that the stripping back of winter allows us to see truths about God and consequently about ourselves, things that are harder to see in other seasons of life. If we allow them to, this stripping back and slowing down gives us the opportunity to experience God's love in new and tangible ways, right in the midst of the cold and dark of winter. Crucially, it's His loving presence that will strengthen us to endure the cold and dark of winter, and that will, in time, heal us too. In God's hands, seasons of loss can be turned into seasons of growth. The fruit of a winter season walked with God is wisdom; the ability to live life well. But as I

---

[8] Andy Raine, *Celtic Daily Prayer Book One: The Journey Begins* (William Collins, London, 2015), p191.

am learning, wisdom doesn't run – it, or rather He, walks. Jesus is the only truly wise person ever to have lived, and His invitation to us is not to run with Him but to walk with Him.

Walk with me

So, this is my invitation to you to walk with me through winter. To begin with, I will share our story of walking through the loss of six children, five through miscarriage and the death in labour of our first child, Libby.

Then, using the metaphor of winter, I will talk about what our winter felt like, from the pain and heartbreak to the loneliness and isolation that it caused.

One of the realities of faith is how often God calls us to hold two seemingly opposite things together – things that, at first glance, look paradoxical.

This is the case when we walk through seasons of loss. As followers of Jesus, we are called to walk the path He walked. This means we will experience pain and loss, and rather than running from them or denying their reality, we must acquaint ourselves with infirmity (see Isaiah 53:3). To be acquainted with something or someone means to know them. In the Bible, the word translated 'knowledge' does not mean head knowledge; it means relational and experiential knowledge. It implies intimacy: Adam 'knew his wife Eve, and she conceived and bore Cain' (Genesis 4:1). When seasons of pain and loss come in our lives, we need to allow ourselves to experience the reality of the pain and heartbreak they cause. We need to be able to brave the elements of winter, and rather than trying to escape winter in our rush to spring, we must learn how to walk with Jesus through these seasons with honesty and authenticity. We need to know that this ability to 'face down the reality' of our situations is a powerful act of faith.

However, as author William Brodrick movingly articulates, as people of faith we are called to be 'candles burning between hope and despair, faith and doubt, life and death, all the opposites'.[9] Faith requires that we hold heartbreak and hope together. At the same time as being realistic about the pain, we need to know how to hold on to hope. Just as we can use the practice of *hygge* to help us embrace the natural season of winter, I believe that we can create a form of *hygge* that will help us walk through our winter seasons of loss. I have called this '*hygge* for the heartbroken'. Essentially, this is a set of practices that I found hugely helpful when walking through my winter season. They helped me to create intimacy with God, to know His loving presence within all the heartache and pain. As a result, I was able to experience love, peace and joy in the bleakest of winters. Against all the odds, I witnessed God prepare the soil of my soul for new life. The new life of His Kingdom.

As we set out together, I want to say that this is not a journey I have finished; it is not a season I have forever left behind or moved on from. This is one of the myths about grief, the idea that you will get over it. It's nearly nine years since our daughter Libby died and I am still on this journey of loss; grief is multilayered, and at different times along this journey I have found myself back in its raw depths.

My dad is a keen fell walker. Growing up, whenever I went walking with him, he would take his Wainwright guides with him. In these books, Alfred Wainwright would share his own experience of walking a particular fell as well as provide detailed guidance to others of the route to follow, including potential hazards and pitfalls. I would love it if this book were to become a 'walkers guide' of sorts, a guidebook for walking through winter seasons of loss. In the pages that follow, you'll find not only our story but also, at the end of each chapter, 'walk it out' tips. These give suggestions of how you can put the contents of the chapter into practice in your winter journey. To make the most of these sections, you might like to have a journal beside

---

[9] William Brodrick, quoted in *Celtic Daily Prayer Book Two: Further Up and Further In* (William Collins, London, 2015), p905.

you as you read so that you can engage with these practical suggestions.

I don't know why you have picked up this book. Perhaps you are walking a very similar path to ours, one of baby loss or infertility. Or maybe you find yourself in the winter season for a different reason, perhaps the death of a loved one, the loss of a marriage through divorce, the loss of health through a chronic or terminal illness, or the loss of a job. Maybe your child has a severe learning disability, and you are coming to terms with the impact that this will have on all the 'rites of passage' in life that they (and you) might never get to experience.

Maybe you're not in winter right now but, without wishing to depress you, one thing I do know is that as surely as winter follows autumn each year, loss is inevitable in our lives. None of us gets to escape it; eventually, we will all find ourselves walking our own winter journey. If this is where you find yourself, I hope this book will help you to prepare for winter.

As well as personally experiencing pain and loss, we will all know people who are in the middle of challenging times. The wise vicar who counselled us after the death of Libby very movingly reflected, 'When I became a vicar I was ushered into other people's pain, and I quickly learnt that behind every door is a person in pain.' Supporting people in their suffering can be a daunting prospect. 'What do I do? What can I say that will help?' My prayer is that this book will give you an insight into what it feels like to walk through winter and so help you support and walk alongside friends who are walking this path.

Most importantly, though, I pray that this book is not just more information – another set of ideas or, worse still, an additional burden of things you feel you need to do. Instead, I hope that through the pages of what follows you will have a fresh revelation of the God who loves you more than any of my words could ever describe, whose love is not contingent on what we do or don't do, or on the circumstances of our lives. This is so important because it is the revelation of God's love that will transform our situations. As the Franciscan monk and teacher Richard Rohr says, 'Ideas inform us, but love forms us.'[10] It is through accepting Jesus' invitation to walk with Him and learn from Him that we will be able to experience God's love in the midst of winter, and so dare to set out into the inhospitable conditions and to walk on through them, to find meaning and hope.

---

[10] Richard Rohr and Andreas Ebert, *The Enneagram: A Christian Perspective* (Crossroad Publishing, US, 2018), p xxii.

30

Our winter's tale

Hope deferred makes the heart sick.

Proverbs 13:12

The Oxford Dictionary defines winter as the coldest season of the year. In the northern hemisphere it runs from December to February, and in the southern hemisphere from June to August. Interestingly, if you look at the origins of the word 'winter', it probably literally means 'the wet season'.[11] I can relate to this: as I write, I am looking out onto a grey, cold and wet winter's day and I am very grateful for my warm study.

I often remark to family and friends that I love the changing seasons. I appreciate the reminder from nature that while it might feel like I am stuck in a particular season in my life, I won't stay there forever. The season will change. I enjoy the variety that comes with the changing seasons.

However, unlike the seasons of nature, the seasons of our lives do not follow a regular or sequential pattern. Our lives are complex and multifaceted, which means that we can find ourselves in several different seasons in different areas of our lives all at the same time. Moreover, the seasons of our lives rarely track with the seasons of the natural world.

---

[11] Online Etymological Dictionary, https://www.etymonline.com/word/winter (accessed 5th November 2020).

I was fortunate enough not to have to face winter seasons too early in life. I grew up in a Christian home where I never had cause to doubt my parents' love for me. I have lots of good friends, and I have always been physically fit and healthy. I have also had the privilege of studying at some of the best universities in the world. Then, in 2006, I married the most wonderful man who is a daily reminder to me of God's love and grace. In many ways, I lived (and still live) a life that is very sheltered from the suffering and poverty that is a daily reality for many. To use the seasonal metaphor of this book, I have lived a lot of my life in spring and summer seasons.

In 2009, three years after we were married, Jon and I decided 'the time was right' and wanted to start a family. Everyone who has been on this journey will know the hope and excitement with which you embark. I am an optimist by nature, so I had never really given much thought to the possibility that I might not be able to have children. In many ways, I was very naive. I assumed that when I decided I was ready, I would be able to. And so, we jumped on board the monthly roller coaster that is trying to conceive. Each month would start with the hope that perhaps this could be the one, then the waiting, and ultimately disappointment when my period arrived.

One month became two, three, then four… but that's OK, that's completely normal, right? Seven months in I was getting impatient, and, as my family will tell you, patience isn't one of my virtues. Just to add to the 'fun', my body was also playing tricks on me, in that every month leading up to my period I would feel nauseous, making me wonder whether this was the beginning of morning sickness. As it turned out, no, it wasn't; it was just one of the many and varied symptoms of pre-menstrual syndrome. Don't you just love hormones?!

I came to loathe pregnancy tests. So many months I would delay doing a test because I didn't want to be disappointed – if I didn't do a test then I could live for a few more days with the hope that I might be pregnant. But, eventually, my natural impatience would get the better of me, and I would do a test because I needed to know.

Anyone who has been through a similar journey will know all about this process. I would shut myself away in the bathroom to wee on the little stick and then sit and wait, with my heart racing, for the tiny window on the test stick to tell me my fate. Those three minutes of sitting in the bathroom, waiting, always seemed like the longest minutes of my life. It seems ridiculous that a little diagnostic stick can cause both so much pleasure and so much pain. Over the six years of our winter journey, I lost count of the number of times I emerged from the solitude of the bathroom with my hopes dashed for another month.

Then, in May 2010, I had the joy of the little window displaying the 'pregnant' message.

Jon and I were excited and started to think about what it would be like to be parents. Traditionally, during these early weeks, couples don't tell people that they are expecting a baby. For several reasons, I have never really understood this. Firstly, these initial weeks of pregnancy are when, as a pregnant woman, you often feel at your worst with tiredness and nausea, and yet you have to keep it to yourself. Secondly, the good news that you are expecting a baby is something that you want to share with people. I appreciate that people don't share this news because things are so uncertain during this period; it is the time in a pregnancy where the risk of miscarriage is highest. But I do wonder whether in some way we have come to believe that if we don't allow ourselves to get too excited at this point, it will make miscarriage easier to deal with. Are we hoping in some way to protect ourselves emotionally?

In my experience, this approach has only served to belittle the impact of miscarriage on couples. It has perpetuated the lie that the loss of a baby early in pregnancy is not that big a deal. Worse still, it has created a taboo around talking about miscarriage. If you haven't told people you were pregnant, how can you then tell them that you've lost a baby they didn't even know existed?

Yet the reality is that when a couple lose a baby through miscarriage, they need their friends more than ever. I was about to experience the truth of this. Rather than entering into a summer season of fulfilment and the busyness of preparing to be parents, we were thrown into the beginning of what would turn out to be a six-year-long winter.

At ten weeks pregnant, I started bleeding. We had a late-night trip to the local Accident and Emergency department where we were told it was probably nothing to be concerned about but to come back for a scan in the morning. After a sleepless night worrying, but also desperately trying to hold on to the hope that bleeding is not always a sign that something is wrong, we returned to a hospital ward I would come to know better than I would want to – the Early Pregnancy Unit. The waiting room of this ward was full of couples in similar situations to us. Some were anxiously waiting to go in for a scan; others were sitting in silent shock or quietly weeping, having been told that they had lost their precious baby and were now waiting to be given their options for 'management' of this loss.

Then we were called into the clinic room. I will always vividly remember the anxious silence as the sonographer applied cold jelly and rolled the ultrasound probe over my tummy, all the while staring intently at the screen. Then she turned to me and said the words that we had dreaded hearing: 'I'm so sorry, but…'

It turned out that I was experiencing a missed miscarriage. If I started this journey with a lot of naivety, step by step this was knocked out of me as I was sadly forced to learn a whole load of new medical terms, of which this was the first. A missed miscarriage is when the foetus dies but the mother's body fails to recognise this and continues to produce pregnancy hormones. In our case, our baby had probably died a couple of weeks before I had any symptoms.

Having received this heartbreaking news, we then had to decide what to do in terms of how to manage this miscarriage. I could just go home and 'wait for nature to take its course', or

I could speed up the process by using a pessary. I chose the third option, which was to have the miscarriage surgically managed in a procedure called the 'evacuation of the retained products of conception', or ERPC. I have always hated this terminology as it reduces precious babies to little more than cells that need removing. Although I was only a few weeks pregnant, I had already bonded with my baby and started imagining what he or she might be like. I had carried him or her with me twenty-four hours a day, seven days a week. Jon and I had even given the baby a nickname. He or she was not the retained products of conception, but our child.

I took this miscarriage hard. It was like someone had taken the little flickering candle of hope and snuffed it out. As Proverbs 13:12 says, 'Hope deferred makes the heart sick.' I was heartsick. I also felt a real sense of emptiness; this is hard to explain, but when you have begun to share your body with another little life which is then abruptly and prematurely removed, it leaves a real sense of physical emptiness.

However, we resolved to keep going. We knew the statistics: one in four pregnancies end in miscarriage.[12] We were just unlucky; perhaps next time it would be better. So we climbed back on board the roller coaster. Month after month went by with nothing, until after a year we decided that perhaps we should go to the doctor and just check that there was nothing wrong.

In the spring of 2011, we started 'fertility investigations'. One of the things that I hated most about our whole journey was how invasive the medical tests and procedures were; my body was not my own. These days I don't even bat an eyelid at the thought of a smear test – it's nothing in comparison to some of what I went through.

---

[12] Miscarriage Association,
https://www.miscarriageassociation.org.uk/information/miscarriage/
(accessed 5th November 2020).

As part of fertility assessment, I had blood tests to check my hormone levels and Jon had his 'little swimmers' checked. None of these tests suggested that there was anything untoward going on.

I also went through a hysterosalpingogram (doesn't that just roll off the tongue?), or HSG for short. This test checks out the female 'plumbing'. Are the fallopian tubes open? What does the uterus look like and does it have any fibroids, polyps or scar tissue? And so, I found myself in another clinic room with a radiographer staring intently at another screen before turning to me with not-so-great news, this time that I had an unusually shaped uterus, known as a unicornuate uterus.

Did you think unicorns were mythical creatures? Well, I'm here to tell you otherwise. We do exist, but we are very rare. Only one in every 4,000 women is one.[13] I joke, but it's not a laughing matter. The radiographer told me that I have a congenital abnormality, which means my uterus is only half the size it should be and that I only have one fallopian tube. Oh, and I might also only have one kidney.

This was shattering for me, and, of course, I had a whole load of questions. Would I be able to conceive again? Would I have a higher rate of miscarriage? Could I carry a baby to full term? The radiographer could answer none of these questions and referred me back to my gynaecologist.

What do we all do nowadays while we wait to see a doctor? We spend hours on Google, generally scaring ourselves to death. I was no different, except that with a biomedical background and access to scientific journals, I was able to glean some slightly more reliable information.

As well as going on a desperate hunt for information, I dealt with a real sense of failure; I felt like I was failing as a woman.

---

[13] D Reichman, M R Laufer, B K Robinson, 'Pregnancy outcomes in unicornate uterti: a review' (*Fertility and Sterility*, Volume 91, April 25, 2008), pp1886-1894.

Being told that my uterus was in some way defective made me feel less female, less womanly. The uterus is more than just a part of the female anatomy; it has a powerful connection to our sense of womanhood and what it means to be female. On top of this, I also felt that I was failing Jon – the problem was with me; he had chosen a dud, as it were.

When I did finally manage to speak to my doctor, he was a little more optimistic and reassured me that my abnormality did not mean I couldn't conceive and carry a child to full term. However, he did say that if or when I was pregnant again, I would need to be under consultant care and treated in a unit that specialises in looking after women with medical complications. While the news that I had a uterine abnormality was not the best (to put it mildly), nor what Jon and I were expecting, we resolved to focus on the positives. At least we would go into any future pregnancy armed with this information and knowing that we would receive specialist medical care.

Not that long after this diagnosis (October 2011), I fell pregnant again, and we began the journey of pregnancy with a heady mix of hope and excitement tempered with anxiety and fear. I have heard other women talk about 'toilet terror' when they are in the early stages of pregnancy and have experienced miscarriage previously. Toilet terror was a reality for me in this pregnancy. I would delay going to the toilet for as long as possible until I was absolutely bursting because I didn't want to go to the loo and discover that I was bleeding. I also found myself second-guessing all the aches and pains, desperately hoping that they were just the normal aches of the uterus stretching, not the beginnings of miscarriage.

Waiting for your first scan when you have previously had a miscarriage feels like the longest wait of your life. Because of my 'weird womb', I had to wait slightly less time than other women and was booked in for an ultrasound scan and consultant appointment in the high-risk unit of our local hospital at nine weeks of pregnancy. So one December afternoon in 2011, we found ourselves sitting in another clinic waiting room. I have certainly done my tour of hospital waiting rooms. One thing they all had in common was how warm they were. I used to find myself carrying a trail of unnecessary layers of clothes around from one clinic room to the next.

As is so often the case in these units, this particular clinic was running late. To move things along, I was initially seen and scanned by a registrar (junior doctor) who then handed me over to my consultant. I was not in the room as part of this handover, but it took place in the next-door room, so Jon and I heard the full conversation. Clearly, both doctors were analysing the ultrasound image, as my consultant said, 'Did you spot the vanishing twin?' The registrar confirmed she had seen this but had chosen not to tell us as it was potentially upsetting news that we didn't need to know.

Vanishing twin syndrome is a type of miscarriage where two embryos start to develop, but one then stops. Unlike a normal miscarriage, there are no symptoms for vanishing twins as you are still pregnant. Instead, the aborted embryo or foetus is reabsorbed into the body of the mother. Data on how common vanishing twins are is hard to come by because it often happens before a woman has her first scan at twelve weeks, after the embryo has been reabsorbed. It could be that our 'vanishing twin' was picked up because I had a slightly earlier scan. To be honest, at this point, rather than feeling any sense of loss over this baby, I felt relieved because, with my smaller uterus, a twin pregnancy would not have been a good idea. It sounds brutal, but I still had one healthy baby, and that was more than enough for me. It's only in the light of what then happened that I have reflected on this and been able to admit that this was another baby that we lost.

As part of this appointment, my consultant told me that he was not overly concerned about my uterine abnormality. He reassured me that plenty of women with a unicornuate uterus have perfectly normal pregnancies. In contrast to what my gynaecologist had told us, this consultant said that I was not a high-risk case and didn't need to be seen regularly in his clinic.

He told me that he would still see me a couple of times during my pregnancy but that my community midwife would be more than able to support me.

With hindsight, I have found myself going over and over this appointment and questioning whether I was too trusting of my consultant. Should I have asked more questions? At the time, I was working in neonatal research at the same hospital, so I had a chat with one of my colleagues that I trusted. He reassured me that my consultant was clinically very well respected. If I didn't trust him, whom would I trust?

I loved being pregnant and thanked God on an almost daily basis for the blessing that it was. I loved how, after several years of waiting, I was finally able to buy some maternity clothes, watch my body change shape and be proud of my growing bump.

I had my twenty-week scan, and all looked good, so we started to buy all the baby stuff, cots, prams, buggies, cute babygrows. We decorated a room – in neutral colours as we had decided not to find out what sex our baby was.

I had regular check-ups with the midwife during which she measured my bump and monitored the baby's heartbeat. I also had a couple of appointments with my consultant, but these seemed to be fairly routine. Like the midwife, my consultant measured my bump. At no time were any of these measurements outside normal parameters, so no one ever felt the need for further ultrasound scans after twenty weeks. I had had my final consultant appointment at thirty-six weeks, when he discharged me from his care with the words, 'We have tried to make you abnormal, but you have had a very straightforward pregnancy.' I finished work, and Jon and I looked forward to welcoming our new little person into the world. We were ready to enter this new season of life.

On 2nd July 2012, at thirty-eight weeks pregnant, I was concerned that my waters were breaking, so we went to the hospital. The midwife connected me to a cardiotocograph (CTG) machine that monitored the baby's heart rate and my uterine contractions. The midwife assured us that the baby's heartbeat was strong. While my waters hadn't broken, the CTG trace did show that I was in early labour. The midwife sent me home to let labour progress, which it did during the night. As our hospital was a good forty-five minutes away from home, I was determined to be in fully established labour before heading back to the hospital; I did not want them turning me away again!

By seven o'clock the following morning, I was having contractions every three minutes. We drove to the hospital with a sense of nervous excitement; today was the day that our lives would change forever. After three years of waiting and nine months of pregnancy, we were going to meet our first child.

In my naivety, like a lot of other first-time mums, I had put a birth plan together. As many women will tell you, whatever your plan is, it often goes out the window once you are in labour. Having told yourself you wouldn't have an epidural, you find yourself begging for one! Part of my birth plan was to give birth in the Midwife Led Unit (MLU) of our local hospital as several of my friends had told me this would be a more relaxed experience.

When we arrived at the hospital we went up to this unit. By this point I was in quite a lot of pain. As part of the initial checks, they asked me to lie down on the bed, which any woman who has been in labour will tell you is the last thing you want to do. It just makes the pain worse. A student midwife was tasked with finding the baby's heartbeat. When she couldn't find it, I wasn't particularly worried; I knew which way round the baby was, and as far as I could tell she was looking in the wrong place. I mentioned this to the senior midwife, and she then took over. I only really started to panic when she couldn't find a heartbeat either. At this point, the midwife called for a consultant with an ultrasound machine. After a couple of minutes of yet another clinician staring silently at the screen of an ultrasound machine, we were given the news that no parent ever wants to hear... 'I'm so sorry, but your baby has died.'

Lots of people have asked me what I thought, how I felt at this point. To be honest, my first thought was, 'Lord, if my baby has died, then I want to die too.'

Then I realised that I would have to give birth to a baby that was not alive. I begged the consultant to give me a C-section, but she refused, explaining that, for the sake of my future fertility, it was vital to deliver normally. I remember being outraged at this. 'What future fertility? I am never putting myself in this position again.'

Rather than a C-section, the doctors administered an epidural to numb the physical pain. After this, I think I went into autopilot. I don't remember very much about the day; I was in shock. Emotional intelligence experts would call it an amygdala hijack: my rational brain went into shutdown. Even if I wanted to, I was not capable of rationally or cognitively processing what was going on. I just did what I needed to do to get through it.

What I do remember, however, is feeling a sense of calm and peace – which was entirely at odds with the situation and the last thing I should have felt. I remember asking Jon to put worship music on during my labour. During my pregnancy, I had talked with Christian friends about witnessing to midwives and nurses during labour. I remember still being concerned to witness to them about God even when it had all gone wrong. As a result of this desire, Jon and I were intentional about the way we treated all the staff. We wanted them to see that even in the darkest time, God was still present.

In the days and weeks afterwards, I often found myself asking, 'Where was God that day?' The answer is that through the Holy Spirit He was in me, strengthening and sustaining me and giving me 'the peace of God, which surpasses all understanding' (Philippians 4:7). There is no way I would have got through all that we went through without God's presence and strength.

At 8:50pm on 3rd July 2012, our beautiful daughter Libby was born asleep. I will always remember the silence, the absence of the newborn cry. I also remember being very concerned about what she might look like; I had never seen a dead body and didn't know what to expect. I was worried that she had suffered as she died and was concerned that in some way this distress and suffering would show on her face. But when our midwife gave her to me, I looked down at her, and she looked like any other beautiful newborn baby. She looked like she was just asleep, although the heartbreaking reality was that she would never wake up. I would never see her little eyes open and stare into mine with the recognition that I was her mummy. Jon and I talk about it being the worst hello ever. We were devastated.

To add to it all, I then ended up in surgery as I had a retained placenta. I gave Libby to Jon with the instructions to keep her warm. One of the things that I hated most was that, when she was born, Libby was warm; but she would get cold, and, unlike other babies, she would never be warm again. I wanted this moment where she was still warm to last as long as possible.

Jon was left holding Libby and was told that surgery wouldn't take long. In fact, it took more than two hours. I will always remember the look of relief on his face when he was finally allowed into the theatre to see me. He has reflected since on the anguish he felt as he sat in the delivery room holding Libby while she went cold in his arms, and at the same time worrying about me and fearing that he was going to lose us both. This is an experience that no father should ever have to endure.

It was at this point that we had our first interaction with Sands (Stillbirth and Neonatal Death Society), a fantastic charity working to support anyone affected by the death of a baby. As well as providing practical support through its website, befriending network and local Sands support groups, it also funds research into how to support those affected.[14] As a result,

---

[14] Stillbirth and Neonatal Death Society (Sands)
https://www.sands.org.uk/ (accessed 2nd December 2020).

over the last couple of decades, the care that bereaved parents receive while in hospital has improved hugely. In the past, when a baby was stillborn, the child was 'whisked away' and parents often never saw their baby, let alone were allowed to hold him or her. Bereaved mothers were then placed on regular maternity wards full of healthy newborns. When discharged, parents did not have a chance to hold any kind of funeral or thanksgiving service for their baby. All of this served to perpetuate the lie that their dead baby was never a person. It was almost as if the baby had never existed.

After Libby was born, Jon and I were transferred to a dedicated bereavement flat in the hospital funded by Sands. This was such a gift as it meant Jon was able to stay with me and we could spend as much time with Libby as we liked. No one was in a rush to discharge us home. We also had an incredible team of specially trained bereavement midwives caring for us.

We spent two days in this flat. Our family came to visit, and all had a chance to hold Libby. We have photos of her with members of our immediate families and with us, which are so precious. We even took videos of us holding her and talking to her, which although are too painful to watch most of the time, are really important to have. In many ways, I didn't want to leave the hospital because I knew I would have to leave Libby behind. I can't put into words how hideous it was when, two days after Libby was born, we said goodbye to her and walked out of the maternity unit with empty arms and broken hearts.

We then had to go through the ordeal of choosing a place to bury Libby and organising a thanksgiving service for her – I could never call it a funeral. When I look back now, I don't know how we survived those early days. I think the best way to describe it was that we were sleepwalking through our lives, as none of it seemed real.

My body was a daily painful reminder of all that we had lost; I had a post-pregnancy body but no baby. I wanted to be able to hang a sign around my neck that said, 'I look this way because

I have been pregnant, but my baby died.' Our house was full of cards from friends and family, but they were not the kind of cards I wanted. I wanted 'Congratulations on your new baby' cards, not 'I'm so sorry for your loss' cards.

On top of this, we had a room in the house that we couldn't go into. The door was shut on what should have been Libby's bedroom and remained that way for nine months. We only opened this door when we packed up the room as part of moving house.

We also had to go back to the hospital for a follow-up appointment with my consultant. At this appointment, we found out that Libby had died because she had something called Intrauterine Growth Restriction (IUGR), which meant that she was too weak to survive labour. My consultant informed us that if Libby's growth restriction had been diagnosed, I would not have been allowed to go into labour but would have had a C-section. Had this happened, Libby would have been in the Special Care Baby Unit (SCBU) for a bit, but ultimately there is no reason why she would not have been a perfectly healthy little girl. This news was another body blow. Rather than Libby's death being one of those hideous but unavoidable tragedies, we know that it was preventable. I also found myself questioning the seemingly obvious connection between a baby whose growth was restricted and a uterus that is half the size it should be, a link my consultant told me there were no data to back up.

In the immediate aftermath of Libby's death, I remember thinking to myself that I was never going to put myself in the position where I could lose like that again. I was not going to have another baby. Jon and I would look at other ways of having a family, perhaps through adoption, but I would not put myself through that again. However, very quickly this changed; the desire to have children of our own was so powerful that it overrode my fears.

We also felt really strongly that God had given us a promise that we would have our own children. When I was pregnant, we had chosen Libby as the name for a girl because, as a derivative of Elizabeth, it means 'God's promise'. While I was in labour, knowing that our baby had died, Jon and I had a conversation about whether we would still use the name we had chosen. Within minutes of our baby girl's birth, we agreed that we should stick with the name Libby. We both felt that she was God's promise to us that we would have other children; she had shown us that we could have a baby.

So we resolved to keep going, to put ourselves back on the monthly roller coaster. It took us another two years and three further miscarriages, two very early and one at eleven weeks, followed by two failed IVF attempts, before, in September 2014, we conceived our son Charlie. Thanks to the excellent care that I received during pregnancy, he was born safe and well at full term in May 2015. But that is a story for another day.

There you have it, the blow-by-blow account of our winter season of loss. While it's unlikely that your experience of loss, of winter seasons in life, is circumstantially the same as mine, there are similarities to all seasons of loss. It's to this I now want to turn as I talk about how our winter season felt.

Walk it out

- Although it's hard, there is real value and healing to be found in journalling the details of our experiences of loss. If you have never done this, you might want to put aside some time to start.

The bleak midwinter

In the bleak midwinter, frosty wind made moan,

Earth stood hard as iron, water like a stone;

Snow had fallen, snow on snow, snow on snow,

In the bleak midwinter, long ago.

Christina Rossetti, 1872

When speaking about the natural world, the word 'bleak' means inhospitable, barren, cold or miserable. By the middle of the winter, nature is at its bleakest. The hedgerows make slim pickings for birds foraging for seeds, the trees have lost all their leaves, and the fields are either frozen solid or a boggy mess. All in all, it's a pretty inhospitable time, not only for birds and animals but also for us humans.

Charlie is a little boy who loves being outside, and one of the things I dislike about winter is how much effort it takes to get us both ready to brave the elements. There are so many layers to fight our way into (and to convince Charlie that he needs!). Then there are the big boots that are as tricky to get off as they are to put on. To be honest, I would often much rather be huddled inside by the fire with a good book.

If I were to ask you for adjectives to describe winter, what would spring to mind? Perhaps the words 'cold' and 'dark' would be in there. If, like me, you live in the UK, then 'wet' and 'long' might also feature. I'm sure there would be some positive adjectives too; I love stepping outside on a cold, clear evening and feeling the cold air awaken my senses, helping me feel truly alive. I find myself turning to gaze at the dazzling beauty of a full moon or staring at the stars and being reminded of the vastness of the cosmos. Or what about those evenings in with friends and family, safe and warm while a storm rages outside?

We'll come to these, but for now I am going to be looking at the bleaker aspects of winter.

Cold

Winter seasons in our lives can feel cold because they often bring with them a sense of isolation. This loneliness and isolation manifest in three different ways: physical isolation, social isolation and spiritual isolation.

Physical isolation

When a loved one dies or leaves, it can bring an intense sense of physical loneliness. Perhaps you have experienced the loss of your partner either through death or divorce, and you now find yourself living alone. One of the real gifts of marriage or having a partner is companionship. Someone to talk to about how your day has been, or another person to turn the lights on, so you don't always go back to an unlit house. Someone to curl up next to in the evening while watching TV or reading a book. Or the joy of having someone with whom you can simply sit in companionable silence. Just the physical presence of someone else with you, witnessing and sharing your life.

Or maybe you have had a close relative die, such as a brother or sister, or a close friend. While you might not have lived with them recently, if ever, their death still brings physical isolation as you no longer get to experience their physical presence with you. You'll never hear them laugh or get to hug them again.

Personally, in the weeks after Libby died, I remember feeling intense physical loneliness whenever I went out on my own. In any behavioural profiling I have ever done, I sit right on the introvert/extravert boundary, so although I love being with people, I also need my own space. One of the things that I love doing is going to a favourite coffee shop and disappearing into a book. In these situations, I am alone but not lonely. After Libby died, I found it hard to be on my own in these kinds of settings. For the whole nine months I had carried Libby I had never been on my own; she had always been with me. After she died, I couldn't enjoy spending time on my own because I should not have been on my own. Even if I didn't have the company of another adult, I should always have had my baby with me.

The coronavirus pandemic brought with it a sense of physical isolation, the scale of which we have never seen. The governments of many countries put nationwide lockdowns in place, with people confined to their homes and only allowed to leave to buy food or medicine or to travel to work if it was not possible to work from home. All elderly and medically vulnerable people were advised not to leave their homes at all for the foreseeable future, leaving them reliant on family and friends to buy their food and collect essential supplies. This is a population of people who can be prone to loneliness even at the best of times.

Throughout the coronavirus pandemic, we became reliant on social media and videoconferencing in order to stay in touch with those we know and love who didn't live with us. While this was amazing and meant that we were less isolated than we might otherwise have been, nothing replaces seeing people 'in the flesh'. We all know the power of physical touch, the comfort that we can give or receive through a hug. For those who live on their own, this was incredibly hard, as there was no one with whom they were allowed to be in physical contact.

For those whose loved ones died during this time, there was the terrible reality of having to grieve alone. Just when they needed their extended family and friends most, they were not allowed to visit.

Social isolation

As well as physical isolation, winter seasons often bring with them a sense of social isolation, of being out of step with everyone around you. Perhaps you are living with a chronic health condition, and all you see around you are physically fit and able people. Or maybe you're struggling financially, and it feels like everyone else around you has money you don't have.

For me, during our winter season, it felt like the whole world was having babies. I lost count of the number of friends, family members and work colleagues I had to congratulate (through gritted teeth) on being pregnant. Baby showers were a no-go zone; to be honest, they still are. As many of our friends and family were having children, social occasions became (understandably) very child orientated. Attending family or friends' gatherings took an enormous amount of emotional energy. We were surrounded by precisely what we longed for and had been stolen from us.

More than this, meeting new people at these kinds of gatherings was a conversational minefield. I always dreaded the 'Do you have children?' question. How was I to answer it? Saying no was a lie, but saying yes meant having a rabbit-in-headlights moment, with the other person suddenly put on the spot and not knowing exactly how to respond when I revealed something of my story. I got to the point of being so troubled by this question that, with Jon, I worked out a formulaic answer to it. The formula worked like this: if I was talking to someone I was unlikely ever to meet again, the answer would be, 'No, we don't.' If I were likely to see the person again or become friends with them, I'd say, 'Yes, we have a daughter, but sadly she died at birth.' Then I'd very quickly move the conversation on. I still use this formula for the related question, 'Is Charlie your only child?'

Your 'minefield' question is likely to be different to mine – perhaps, 'Do you have a partner?' or, 'What do you do for work?' If this resonates with you, I would highly recommend that you think about having a rote answer to it, something you can say which means you stay in control of the conversation and can move it on.

Spiritual isolation

As well as feeling physically and socially 'out in the cold', I felt spiritually very lonely too. I felt as though God had disappeared. I will come back to this later, when I talk about the darkness of winter seasons.

Sadly, many Christians walking through seasons of loss can also find going to church a lonely experience. If you are single, or married but childless, this may come from the focus of many churches on families. Or if you are struggling financially or with an addiction, it can be hard to be open and honest in this setting, perhaps out of fear that others will judge you. Sadly, there can be a real pressure to 'have it all together' and a sense that if you don't, you are spiritually failing in some way.

Wet

In the UK, the winter of 2019/2020 was one of the wettest winters on record,[15] which caused significant problems for farmers all over the country as it basically didn't stop raining from October through to March! Very few crops were planted in the autumn, and those that farmers did manage to sow often failed to grow. When it finally 'came dry' in late March, all around where we live farmers rushed to get crops planted in time.

---

[15] Met Office, https://www.metoffice.gov.uk/about-us/press-office/news/weather-and-climate/2020/2020-winter-february-stats (accessed 5th November 2020).

Seasons of loss in our lives are wet because they often bring a lot of tears. One of the books that I had read previously but felt drawn to return to after Libby's death was Canadian writer Wm Paul Young's *The Shack*.[16] This fictional story tells the tale of Mac, a father whose young daughter was murdered by a serial killer in a deserted shack in the woods. In a mysterious letter from 'Papa', Mac is invited back to this shack. With great trepidation, he heads back to the place of his greatest heartbreak. What unfolds is Mac's experience of a weekend spent with the Trinity. It is a powerful story of healing and restoration.

At one point in the book, Mac talks to Papa (God the Father) about hating how often he finds himself crying.[17] I resonated with this; I have never cried as much as I did after Libby died. Our winter season was very wet. I remember talking to Jon one day about how fed up I was with crying; it felt like it was all I had been doing for several years as we walked through one baby loss after another.

Stormy

Winter is also a season of storms. Just as each hurricane is named, the Met Office in the UK has taken to naming winter storms. Over the past couple of years, among others, we have had storms Deirdre, Erik, Ciara, Dennis and Jorge. Storms bring with them high winds and rain, which can cause severe damage to people and properties. Weather forecasters say they name each storm based on the impact it may have and the likelihood of those impacts occurring.[18]

Seasons of loss in our lives can bring with them storms in the form of anger. Anger at how unfair and unjust our situation

---

[16] Wm Paul Young, *The Shack* (Hodder & Stoughton, London, 2008).
[17] Wm Paul Young, *The Shack*, p228.
[18] Met Office, https://www.metoffice.gov.uk/weather/warnings-and-advice/uk-storm-centre/index (accessed 5th November 2020).

seems, or anger at someone or an organisation we feel has let us down badly. Perhaps we're angry with ourselves. Maybe we think we missed a crucial piece of information that could have saved our loved one's life, or perhaps we have convinced ourselves that we didn't work hard enough, which is why our dream career has come crashing down around us.

When Libby died, I was angry with the medical staff who I felt had let us down. I was also angry with myself. Had I missed something that would have saved Libby's life or prevented my miscarriages? And I was angry at the unfairness of it all. Why did it have to be our babies? Most of all, I was angry with God for seemingly allowing it all to happen.

There were several occasions where this anger manifested itself in a storm of angry words. On one memorable occasion, the storm of anger resulted in damage to our property as, while unloading a dishwasher, I threw a plate across the floor of our kitchen. As our kitchen had a tiled floor, the plate smashed into a million pieces. It was briefly really satisfying, but I was finding shards of the broken plate for weeks afterwards!

What's more, going through traumatic loss triggers our body's fight-or-flight response. Essentially, our body is sensing danger and doing whatever is necessary to get us out of the situation. Part of the bodily response is to release the stress hormones adrenaline and cortisol. These hormones raise our heart rate and blood pressure, increase blood sugar and redirect blood away from the digestive system to our muscles. All of this prepares our bodies to either face or flee from the danger. The problem when we are going through something traumatic is that this stress response becomes chronic, and high levels of adrenaline and cortisol in our bodies are known to be associated with health issues like high blood pressure, anxiety, insomnia and digestive problems.

I found that chronically raised levels of adrenaline and cortisol meant that my anger threshold was much lower. Essentially, things that I wouldn't have perceived as a threat were initiating my fight-or-flight response. I found myself getting angry in situations that would never normally have triggered this response in me. What's more, all the adrenaline coursing through my system resulted in heart palpitations, which only served to make me more anxious.

Storms are also noisy. Just think about the noise of the wind and rain during a winter storm. Or think about the opposite – how calm and quiet the world seems when you find yourself in a sheltered spot on a windy day. The same is true of the internal storms we face during winter seasons. The noise of the constant chatter of our fearful and anxious thoughts can be overwhelming and seemingly inescapable.

Long

In contrast to the warm sunny days of summer that seem to be over and gone before we know it, winter often feels like a long season. In the UK, the winter of 2017/2018 went on and on. Unusually, we had our first snowfall in mid-December. This was exciting and had some novelty value, certainly for Charlie, who got to build his first ever snowman. However, by the time the Beast from the East brought snow and freezing temperatures to much of the UK in late February and early March, most people were well and truly done with winter. My birthday is in early March, and my present that year was to wake up to no running water in our house because the pipes had frozen. The country had a brief respite before more snow in the middle of March. By this point, I was on the computer, googling how far south in the world I'd have to fly to get some warm sunshine!

In the same way that winter in the natural world can feel like a long season, the winter seasons of loss in our lives can feel like they will never end. Our winter season of baby loss lasted for six years. I'm aware that for people living with long-lasting issues such as chronic illness, this is not a long period of time. For us, though, these six years felt like they went on and on. I often darkly joked with friends that it was like I was living in

Narnia under the reign of the White Witch, where it's always winter but never Christmas.[19]

When we are involved in something hard, it can feel like time stretches. I regularly experience this phenomenon in my gym classes. A minute seems to last a lifetime when all my muscles are screaming at me to stop!

What is it they say? 'Time flies when you're having fun.' Well, the exact opposite can be true when we are in winter seasons. Time does anything but fly by because life can feel like such hard work. Walking through the pain of loss is exhausting on every level; it is physically, emotionally and spiritually draining. It takes real courage and perseverance to keep going when every step feels so hard.

Another reason that winter seasons feel long is that they are often seasons of waiting. In nature, animals and plants go dormant in winter, waiting for the light and warmth of spring when they will burst into life again. It seems appropriate that, as we enter winter in the northern hemisphere, we also enter the Church season of Advent, which is all about waiting. We look back to the waiting of the nation of Israel for the promised Messiah. And we reflect on the period of waiting we are now in between the first and second comings of Jesus.

When we are waiting for something, it feels like time slows down. This can be for something exciting, like a small child waiting for Christmas and for whom Advent seems interminable. Pretty much every day through Advent, Charlie asks me whether it's Christmas yet.

More seriously, during the coronavirus crisis, the world was waiting, waiting for a vaccine that would allow governments to be able to ease restrictions on daily life.

---

[19] C. S. Lewis *The Lion, the Witch and the Wardrobe* (Geoffrey Bles, London, 1950).

Vulnerability

One of my favourite poems is 'The Lucky Poor' by Eugene Peterson. This poem uses the metaphor of a beech tree in winter to talk about the wisdom of letting things go. Its opening lines talk about how when a beech tree loses its leaves its structural intricacies are revealed.[20] To me, these lines speak of vulnerability. When a beech tree loses its leaves, it is stripped back, and you see the structure underneath which has been concealed by the leaves of summer.

One of the things that seasons of loss can do is make us feel vulnerable. When we have experienced the loss of someone or something that is precious to us, risking our hearts again, allowing ourselves to hope again feels like a scary thing to do. It can in some ways feel more manageable, less scary, not to put yourself 'out there' again. Perhaps you have risked everything trying to create your own business and it all fell down around you. Trying again is likely to feel terrifying. Or maybe a close friend hurt you and you don't want to step out and risk your fragile heart again in a new relationship.

I felt really vulnerable when it came to allowing myself to be pregnant again. Even for those of us who are fortunate enough to live in the developed world with modern healthcare, pregnancy and childbirth are not without risks, and it is a time of physical vulnerability for every woman. In my case, previous losses served to heighten that sense of vulnerability. With each positive pregnancy test, alongside the hope was the fear of losing again.

Opening ourselves up when we have experienced heartbreaking loss makes us vulnerable from a spiritual point of view too. Trusting God again after feeling so let down is not an easy thing to do. When you realise that faith does not protect you from the worst that life can throw at you, what does trust

---

[20] Eugene H Peterson, *Holy Luck* (William B. Eerdmans, Grand Rapids, 2013), p3.

in God look like? And can we allow ourselves to hope that next time will be different?

I'd love to say that during my pregnancy with Charlie I felt a sense of peace, but the truth was that I was anxious throughout. Some Christians encouraged me that, with God, I didn't need to feel afraid, that He was protecting my unborn little boy and me. The problem for me was that I was scared, not of something irrational, but I was afraid because I had experienced one of the worst things of life, and I knew how awful it was. It wasn't that I didn't trust that God would be with me if I were to lose again. Having walked through the death of Libby with Him, I knew that He would be. I just didn't want to be back in that place. I longed for things to be different this time.

Winter seasons are also a time of vulnerability when it comes to personal identity. It is not unusual in the wake of a loss to find yourself asking, 'Who am I?' and struggling to find an answer; this is where I found myself after Libby died. Not only did I lose my daughter, but in a way I lost myself too.

Dark

There are several models of the grieving process; the most famous is probably Elizabeth Kübler-Ross' five stages of grief.[21] However, the model I find more helpful is grief counsellor Lois Tonkin's 'Growing Around Grief'.[22] In this model, we imagine our life as a circle, and grief is a black hole within the circle. In the immediate aftermath of loss, the black hole of grief consumes the whole of our life. Over time, the hole doesn't shrink, but life grows bigger around it so that our circle is now no longer entirely black. Pictorially, we have something resembling a fried egg! There are times when life shrinks back

---

[21] Elizabeth Kübler-Ross, *On Death and Dying: What the Dying have to Teach Doctors, Nurses, Clergy and Their Own Families* (Routledge, 1969).
[22] Lois Tonkin, 'Growing Around Grief – another way of looking at grief and recovery' (*Bereavement Care*, Volume 15 issue 1, 1996), p10.

again, and we feel like we are back in the black hole of grief; for me, the days running up to Libby's birthday are a time every year when life shrinks back again.

The darkness of winter is also disorientating. Think for a minute about the difference between navigating in the daylight compared to night-time. I often speak at evening meetings in little villages around the UK. Finding the venues for these meetings is much more challenging on a dark winter's evening. In the dark, I can't see as far, and the landmarks that I use during the day are lost in the darkness.

One of the ways we combat physical disorientation is through the use of maps. In the same way that we use maps to navigate the physical landscape, we all have a mental map, or a worldview, that we use to navigate our way through the complexities of life. These maps help us orientate ourselves spiritually. As a Christian, my faith is the 'map' that I have used to navigate my way through life.

Seasons of loss can be spiritually disorientating; it can feel like someone has taken our map and torn it to pieces, leaving us feeling lost, anxious and confused. They also generate a lot of questions. Many of the things we think we know about God and how He acts in our lives are thrown into question as a result of our lived experience. How can He be loving and yet allow awful things to happen to us? How is He in control, and how does His protection work? How does prayer work? There were several times during our winter season where I didn't just doubt God's character; I doubted that He even existed. The God I thought I knew seemed to have retreated into the darkness, leaving me lost and alone.

Whether we have faith in God or not, we all have a spiritual map, a worldview that we use to make sense of life. Throughout the coronavirus pandemic, I witnessed a lot of people struggling as the crisis challenged their assumptions about how life should work. People who would not say they had faith found themselves asking the big questions of life. Why is this happening? Who is in control? Who am I? How do I make sense of what is going on? What is the meaning and purpose of life and of my life in particular?

New maps?

When our old maps no longer help us to navigate the terrain in which we find ourselves, our natural response is to look for new maps. But maps on their own are not enough. Guidebooks, like the Wainwright ones my dad was so fond of, are brilliant; the problem is that they don't stop us getting lost. A 'Wilf Walk' is a thing of legend in our family. Generally, any walk with Dad involves getting lost at some point, and that's with his trusty Wainwright book in hand!

Rather than maps and guidebooks, what we really need is a guide – someone who has walked the terrain before and will walk with us to show us the way and help us to avoid the hazards.

The year after Libby died, eight family members and friends joined Jon and me on an expedition to climb Mount Kilimanjaro. Both my parents grew up in Kenya, and my sister and I were born there. As we still have family living there, we have had many trips to Kenya over the years. So climbing Kilimanjaro was something I had always thought about doing. Jon and I had even discussed the possibility. We'd got as far as deciding that we'd need a compelling reason to get us to attempt that kind of challenge. Ideally, it would be to raise money for a charity whose work we were passionate about. At the time of our first conversations, we couldn't think of a cause that would motivate us enough to take on such an expedition. After Libby died, we had our reason for climbing: we would do it for her; we'd raise money for Sands. The mountain is now often referred to as 'Libbymanjaro' in her honour. Now we had the sense of purpose and motivation we needed not only to do all the training but ultimately to make it to the summit.

The key to our success was Jon's mantra that we 'need to do our research'. He repeated this phrase to us all so often that it has since become a family joke. Before embarking on any project, large or small, someone in our family is likely to tell you that you need to 'do some research'! Much as it pains me to say it, Jon was right.

We did our research. We bought guidebooks written by people who had climbed the mountain many times, and we studied which of the routes up the mountain was likely to give us the best chance of all getting to the summit. Most crucial of all, though, was the research Jon did to find us the right team to take us up the mountain. Climbing Kilimanjaro is not something you do on your own. There's a whole army of people who walk and work alongside you to help you achieve your aim. The team includes porters who carry all your bags, camping equipment and food, and experienced guides to lead you up the mountain.

Having climbed many times before, the guides know the terrain like the back of their hands. They also know all the signs of altitude sickness so they can quite literally save your life. Without these people, we would never have made it to the top. They showed us the way, set the pace (a very slow one!), looked out for us, told us to rest when we grew weary, carried the loads that were too heavy for us and encouraged us when we needed it, most memorably in the form of songs in the darkness as we climbed to the summit.

Because they were guiding, protecting and supporting us, it left us free to be fully present to the experience. Rather than burying our heads in maps, or trying to run on too fast, we walked slowly with our heads up, taking in the majesty of our surroundings. Crucially, though, we had to trust them, trust that they were the experts, that they wouldn't get us lost. Trust that they knew the right pace to walk at and how far we needed to walk each day. Interestingly, if anyone in the team asked for details of a climb that was several days away, the guides would bring us back to focus on the present. They gave us just enough information to tackle what was immediately in front of us. We also had to trust that they had our best interests at heart, that they were looking out for us and protecting us. We had to trust them with our lives.

Relying on a guide rather than a map, and asking others to help carry our load, flies in the face of our radically individualistic and self-reliant culture. Rather than make ourselves vulnerable by placing trust in another, we want to be able to go it alone. Instead of allowing someone else to set the pace, we want to control how fast we go. Rather than asking for help, we want to be able to carry our own load. We would much rather have the control that comes from being on our own with a map and all our supplies. God doesn't operate this way, though. Take a look for a moment at the Exodus story.

When God brings the people of Israel out of Egypt, He doesn't give them a map and a truckload of provisions. He guides them in a pillar of cloud by day and of fire by night. He sets the pace of their journey: when the pillar stops, the people stop, and when it moves, they move. And He gives them daily manna for food. God is their guide and their provider.

There are times in life when it's appropriate to rely on a map, and times when it's healthy to walk alone. On a weekend saunter where the landscape is gentle and welcoming and the weather is temperate, it's fine to walk alone. It wouldn't be the end of the world if we were to get lost. But this was not the case on Kilimanjaro. The stakes were too high. What's more, adjusting to the inhospitable landscape and the altitude was enough of a challenge without having to think about navigating and carrying all our supplies.

The bleak, inhospitable landscape of a winter season of loss is not a place to get lost. Before we set out on our journey through winter, we need to go through the same process that Jon and our team went through before our Kilimanjaro expedition. We need to 'do our research'. We need to find guidebooks we can trust, written by people who have taken a similar journey, the wisdom figures of faith both past and present. As you will see in the rest of what follows, I have read my fair share of these kinds of guidebooks. On their own, though, they are not enough. We need a guide who is actually with us as we walk through winter – someone who has walked the path before us, who can show us the way. In short, we need God: Father, Son and Holy Spirit.

What's more, we need to be able to trust God with our lives. We need to trust that He knows the way, that He will protect us, and that His pace is the right one to get us through winter. To be able to do this, we must ask some tough questions about who He is and how He operates in the world.

As well as a guide, we need to do two other things before we brave the elements of winter. Firstly, we need to grow in self-awareness, in the knowledge of who we are. In particular, what are the things about me that might trip me up or mean I don't have the strength or courage to make it through winter? Secondly, we need to know what the point is of making such a perilous journey. Just like Jon and I needed a purpose bigger than our own sense of achievement to get us up Kilimanjaro, we need a sense of purpose and meaning to encourage us to keep going when walking through the pain of loss feels too great.

For all these reasons, it is vital that before we start on our journey through winter, we 'do some research'. We need to ask the big questions concerning who God is, who we are and what possible purpose we can find in all the pain. It is to these questions that I want us now to turn.

Walk it out

- What words come to mind when you think about winter? You might find it helpful to write these down.

- How do these words relate to your own experience of winter seasons in life? How do they describe your own experience of loss?

- Spend some time reflecting on this and talking with God about it.

Part 2

Do your research

Lord, to whom can we go? You have the words of eternal life.

John 6:68

Why is this happening? Who is in control?

My God, my God, why have you forsaken me?

Matthew 27:46

When awful things happen in life, whether we have a faith or not, it's a normal human response to ask lots of questions. We are an inquisitive species and have always asked questions about how the world works and our place in it. Think for a moment of the phase that all young children go through of continually asking 'Why?'. While this can be infuriating for parents, it's a sign of a child's growing interest in the world around them and their desire to know more about it and how it all works.

When faced with the pain of loss, the natural human response is to ask lots of questions such as, 'Why is this happening to me/us?' 'Who is to blame?' 'Who is in control?' 'How can we fix it?' Ultimately, we want to know why something awful is happening so that we can find a way to stop it, which is not wrong. Asking such questions is essential when looking for solutions to a problem.

When Libby died, I felt myself drawn to the biblical book of Job. Job's name is synonymous with suffering, in particular with unwarranted suffering. The writer tells us at the beginning of the book that Job was 'blameless and upright, one who feared God and turned away from evil' (Job 1:1). Job was also a prosperous man, something that, in its original context, people believed signified God's favour and blessing.

The story opens with a discussion between God and Satan (a term that means 'the accuser') about Job. God points Satan to Job saying, 'Have you considered my servant Job? There is no one like him on the earth, a blameless and upright man who fears God and turns away from evil' (Job 1:8). Satan responds that Job only worships God because God has protected him and helped him to prosper. He suggests that if God were to remove his protection, Job would 'surely curse you [God] to your face' (Job 1:11).

What unfolds is the loss of Job's livelihood, family and health. While his wife suggests that Job should 'curse God, and die', through all that he suffers, the author tells us that Job does not sin in what he says (Job 2:9-10). He maintains his integrity and worship of God.

Crucially, maintaining his integrity does not mean that Job doesn't complain about his situation; it doesn't mean that he isn't real with God about how he is feeling. Most of the book (chapters 3–37) describes a to-and-fro conversation between Job and his 'friends' as he and they wrestle with the big questions of why Job is suffering, God's role in it, and what Job should do to make it stop.

Out of control

Behind all these questions, Job's and ours, I believe, is the human desire to feel in control of life. One of the things that seasons of catastrophic loss can do is strip us of our delusion that we are in control. Rather than feeling ordered, predictable and safe, life suddenly feels chaotic, random and scary. In the face of chaos, it is an entirely natural response to grasp for a sense of control.

I would argue that this desire to feel in control extends to our attitude towards God. We want to control Him too. If we can predict how and why God will act (or not), this makes us feel safe. Often the formula works like this: if God is loving, sovereign (by this we mean in control) and all powerful, then either bad things shouldn't happen at all or, if they do, He should act to stop them. What's more, they certainly shouldn't happen to innocent or 'good' people. These assumptions cause many, many people to reject belief in God. Essentially, their view is that suffering and pain are incompatible with a loving, just, sovereign and all-powerful God. In theological language, they reject belief in God because they stumble over the question of theodicy: how can a loving, good and powerful God permit evil?

God is not a control freak

What about the 'Who's in control?' question? Can we answer this? If so, how? While we might, as Christians, get to the point of realising that we are not in control of what happens to us, most of us simply counter with, 'But God is in control.' I understand why we say this; it helps us to feel slightly more secure in a scary situation that is beyond our ability to control or even understand.

The problem is that control is a human construct. It is how we display our power, either over others or over our circumstances. But God's power doesn't work that way. God is not a control freak. God is not in control, but He is sovereign. The difference between these two is vast. As theologian Chris Green so powerfully writes, 'Sovereignty is utterly other than what we have known as control. Control ... violates, overpowers, coerces, masters. Control takes away freedom.'[23]

In contrast, to say that God is sovereign is to affirm that He 'is not at the mercy of what happens in the world ... is not in any rivalry with, much less under the control of, some other

---

[23] Chris E W Green, *Surprised by God: How and Why What We Think about the Divine Matters* (Cascade Books, 2018, accessed from Scribd (www.scribd.com)), p54.

power. God is not and cannot be caught off guard or surprised.'[24] God is sovereign because everything that exists does so because of Him.

While pain, loss and suffering would call into question a notion that God is in control, these same things do not lead us to question God's sovereignty. God is always at work in all circumstances; He is always sovereign. The key is to recognise the presence of God amid our circumstances and find ways of articulating how He is at work, in the best and worst of life.

Changing the question

While it's important that we ask the 'Why?' question, at some point, we must change the question. I realise that this might sound like a cop-out on my part. But, actually, the Bible never answers the 'why' question either. As biblical scholar John H Walton says, many people turn to the book of Job to answer the question of why suffering exists, why they are suffering. But this is the wrong question to come to the book with.

The book of Job is not about the theodicy of God; it does not try to vindicate God. The book of Job is wisdom literature. Therefore, rather than being about why evil exists or who is to blame, or even how God's justice operates, at its heart, the book of Job is about how we interact with God in our suffering. What is our response to mystery? To questions not being answered? Will we choose to trust God when we don't have neat answers? When we don't understand and can't control what is happening to us? When everything is stripped away, will we choose to worship God for who He is, not what we can get from Him?[25]

---

[24] Chris E W Green, *Surprised by God*, p54.
[25] For more on this please see John H Walton and Tremper Longman III, *How to Read Job* (InterVarsity Press Academic, 2015). Or you could watch John Walton's series of YouTube lectures on Job, https://www.youtube.com/watch?v=TGZVjOuxPF4 (accessed 6th November 2020).

If we can make these choices, instead of receiving an explanation from God, what we get is to experience Him in the midst of our pain and loss. In my opinion, we need this far more than we need explanations.

Think back for a moment to the endless questions of a little child and how often the questions are challenging to answer. Usually, this not because we don't know the answer, although in my case Charlie regularly asks questions that I don't know the answer to(!), but because the answer is too complicated for them, as small children, to be able to understand. When I am in a more patient frame of mind, rather than answering, 'Just because,' I will explain to Charlie that he has asked a good question, but it's not one that I can give him an answer to at the moment because the answer is too grown up for him. Most of the time, this answer satisfies him because he trusts me; he knows that I love him, that I'm not trying to hide things from him. He understands that I want the best for him.

When we walk through seasons of pain and loss, we are like the small child asking endless 'why' questions of God. As theologian and pastor Greg Boyd so eloquently articulates, the answers to these questions are probably too complicated for us to understand.[26] It's hard, but one of the things that I learnt through my walk with loss was to be happier with mystery, particularly when it comes to God. I am learning to let go of my need for control, to have formulae about how God works that I can use to get myself out of a situation.

At the same time as we walked through our winter season, I had the privilege of studying with and then later working for Westminster Theological Centre (WTC).[27] While I was working for the college, students would often come to me struggling with their doctrine modules. I understood their pain. When I studied these concepts for the first time, I remember feeling like

---

[26] Gregory A Boyd, *Is God to Blame? Beyond Pat Answers to the Problem of Suffering* (InterVarsity Press, Downers Grove, 2003), pp96-99.
[27] https://wtctheology.org.uk/ (accessed 6th November 2020).

my head was going to explode. For example, how could it be that Jesus is both fully divine and fully human?! Students were frustrated because they didn't feel like they could work it out. My answer generally was that (like Job and his friends) we must wrestle with these big concepts, but ultimately it's also a good thing that we get to the point of mystery. That sense of wow! A sense of awe at the greatness of God. God Himself says, 'For my thoughts are not your thoughts, nor are your ways my ways' (Isaiah 55:8). I, for one, need a God that I can't fathom, that I can't put into a neat box. If I could fully understand God and His ways, then arguably God would not be big enough.

Faith is not about understanding what God is doing or why He is doing it. It's often the opposite. It's the ability to say in the midst of not understanding or knowing what He's doing that we trust Him.[28] To trust Him, we have to know Him deeply and intimately.

Explanations don't help

Our loving heavenly Father knows that even if He could give us an explanation that we would understand, this would not take the pain away. For example, as I explained in a previous chapter, Jon and I have been given a scientific explanation for why Libby died, but this doesn't make her loss any easier. In fact, in some ways, it makes it a lot harder. We know her death was avoidable, which raises a whole load more questions. But more than this, the root of our pain is the fact that Libby is not with us, and no explanation is going to bring her back.

In his book *God on Mute*, founder of the 24-7 prayer movement Pete Greig talks movingly about how when we are

---

[28] Chris Green, 'God's Sovereignty and Our Freedom', Every Day Theology Podcast Episode, 21 May 2020,
https://anchor.fm/everydaytheology/episodes/EP21-Chris-Green--Gods-Sovereignty-and-Our-Freedom-eebf6u (accessed 6th November 2020).

in pain, we are like a small child with chickenpox.[29] As a parent in this situation, you could attempt to explain to the child why they are in pain – give them a lesson on the biology of chickenpox. But this is not going to take the pain away, and the child is highly unlikely to understand the explanation anyway. Instead, what does every parent do? We hold our little ones and love them through the pain and tears. We comfort them with our presence, not with an explanation for their suffering. This is a beautiful metaphor of what our heavenly Father longs to do when we are experiencing the pain of loss. Rather than explaining why it is happening, He longs to hold us and comfort us as we cry and then to lovingly walk with us through our winter season.

Rather than focusing on answering the 'Why is this happening?' question, I want to suggest that we change the question. Instead of 'Why?' we ask 'How?' 'How do I experience God in this season of loss?' 'How can He help me walk on through this tough season of life?'

---

[29] Pete Greig, *God on Mute: Engaging the Silence of Unanswered Prayer* (David C Cook, Lee Lance View, Colorado Springs, 2007), pp59-61.

Walk it out

- What are the questions you find yourself asking God during your winter seasons? How does it feel to think that you might not get answers to these questions?

- What is your response to the idea that God 'doesn't do control'? How does this make you feel?

- Spend some time reflecting on God's words in Isaiah 55:8-9:

  For my thoughts are not your thoughts,
  nor are your ways my ways, says the LORD.
  For as the heavens are higher than the earth,
  so are my ways higher than your ways
  and my thoughts than your thoughts.

Who are You?

Unless the LORD builds the house,

those who build it labour in vain.

Psalm 127:1

One of the programmes Jon and I enjoy watching is *Grand Designs*. The central premise is homeowners battling against the natural elements, local authorities, building contractors and sometimes each other(!) to design and build their dream home. Jon and I used to scorn the couples who appear on this programme and mid-build (when the chaos is at its worst) announce that they are pregnant. My first thought was always, 'Why would you do that to yourself?' I have since had to eat rather a lot of humble pie as this is precisely what happened to us.

Throughout our winter season, Jon and I made a conscious decision not to delay doing things just in case I might be pregnant. So six months after Libby died, when the opportunity came up for us to move to a local farmhouse that needed restoration, we agreed that it would be a good thing for us. It would give us a new project to focus on – other than 'project baby'.

The survey for the house made interesting reading, to say the least. It's not an exaggeration to say that parts of the house were falling down. As the house is listed, it took a long time to get all the necessary planning permissions in place for us to begin work. Then, of course, it took time to line up a builder, all of which is to say that when it finally came to it, the builders started working on the house the day before Charlie was born.

One of the most striking things about our house renovation was how long it took the builders to strip back everything in order to rebuild it. I remember reflecting with Jon at one point that there wouldn't be anything left. The builders stripped our house back to the bare walls – even the roof came off!

However, we knew that although it might look like demolition, actually it was the first step in restoration. The builders were taking great care to strip the house back, to remove all the rotten wood, crumbling plaster, all the structures of the house that made it unsafe, so that when they started to reconstruct our home, they were doing so from a sound foundation. The stripping-back wasn't destruction but a fundamental stage in the reconstruction and restoration of a beautiful building.

Walking through winter seasons of loss can do a similar thing to our way of viewing the world, and whether we are people of faith or not, I believe these seasons strip back our beliefs, our ways of thinking about God. They lead us to question who God is and how He operates in the world. I know for many Christians, myself included, winter seasons can strip faith back to the point where it feels like there is nothing left. We find ourselves living in a rather cold and draughty house that once felt warm, cosy and, crucially, safe, which leaves us feeling very vulnerable.

Author and spiritual director Janet Hagburg says, 'Our image of God will be revealed to us most vividly in times of pain.'[30] How we think about God is crucial to how we face and walk through pain because the God we believe in is the God we experience in our suffering. And crucially, it is only through

[30] Janet O Hagburg, *Who Are You, God? Suffering and Intimacy with God* (At River's Edge Press, Minneapolis, 2013), p13.

experiencing intimacy with God that we will be able to find the strength and perseverance to face and walk through our pain.[31]

I was brought up in a Christian tradition that led me to believe that loss and pain, rather than things to be experienced and journeyed through with God, are problems to be fixed. If something terrible is happening to you, then you just need to pray harder and have more faith, and then you'll see a breakthrough in your situation.

I also grew up with a faith that was all about doing; it was about being busy for God. To be a 'good Christian', I thought I had to tell as many people as I could about God, serve my local church and get involved in social action to help the marginalised and vulnerable. I even took this busyness into my prayer life; for me, prayer was primarily me talking to God, asking Him for the things I needed and interceding (praying) for others.

I want to make it clear that none of these things is wrong; all are needed, and God calls us to action in all these different ways. But they are not and cannot be the sum total of our relationship with Him. In my case, all this busyness for God led me to see my relationship with God as transactional. If I were to do all this stuff for God, He'd bless me with what I wanted. I worked on the same assumption as Job's friends that God's blessing looks like everything going well. If things aren't going well, then it must mean that I have fallen short of the mark, that I have upset God somehow.

As a result of such thinking, for me, God was not an indwelling, loving presence. I viewed Him as an authority figure who was very much 'out there' and separate from me, like a stern father whose love was conditional and whom I had to keep happy by always doing, and ideally being exceptional at what I did.

---

[31] This is unpacked by Janet in a far more eloquent way than I could ever manage in *Who Are You, God?* If you are walking through a season of loss that is challenging your faith, I can't recommend Janet's book highly enough.

My view of God as an authoritarian figure, whose love and approval I had to earn by doing things, meant that my natural reaction when our babies died was to go straight to, 'What can I do?' 'What is wrong in my life that means this is happening to me?' 'What did I do wrong?' 'What needs fixing?' In many ways, I felt like a burden had been placed on me, as the one in pain, to work out why I was suffering and then to fix it. By viewing God in this way, I was robbing myself of intimacy with Him, which was what I needed most in order to face my winter journey.

Much like our house renovation revealed structural weaknesses in our home, this stripping-back of faith caused by seasons of loss often reveals the damaged and broken ways we think about God and the ways He operates in our lives. And while this process can look (and feel) like demolition, this stripping-back is, in fact, the necessary first stage in the godly renovation and restoration of the home that is our faith. For me, rather than 'papering over the cracks', I needed to strip my faith back and examine all my ways of thinking about who God is and His action in my life. I needed to remove the stuff that was rotten and structurally unsound so that my faith would have the strength to withstand winter.

This stripping-back is a painful and demanding process. Sadly, I have heard too many stories of people for whom it ultimately results in the demolition of their faith, mainly because they feel that all these doubts and questions must mean that they are losing their faith. I know I got close to this. I don't think I can overstate how important it is to understand that rather than being an indicator that you are losing your faith, periods of extreme doubt are very normal experiences and fundamental to our ongoing spiritual formation. As Salley Vickers articulates in her novel, *Mr Golightly's Holiday*, while sorrow is a demolition expert, it is also a great architect.[32] I love this picture that deep sorrow can, in God's hands, ultimately lead to the

---

[32] Salley Vickers, *Mr Golightly's Holiday* (Harper Collins, 2007), p191.

reconstruction of a faith and a relationship with God that is more beautiful than what we started with. In the next couple of chapters, I want to share with you something of how God did this in my life through our winter season.

Walk it out

- When you think about God, what words, images or emotions come to mind?

- How has your personal history (your upbringing) affected how you think about God? For example, what were your parents like? How does this affect your ways of thinking about God? If you grew up in church, what impact has this had on your images of God?

- How have the ways you think about God affected how you face winter seasons of loss in your life?

The hidden gem

God did not send the Son into the world to condemn the

world, but in order that the world might be saved through

him.

John 3:17

When the builders stripped our house back, as well as revealing many problems, they also uncovered some beautiful historical features, one of the most precious of these being old wood panelling in one of the bedrooms. When the builders discovered this panelling, Jon and I questioned how anyone could ever have covered up such a beautiful part of the history of the house.

During my period of faith reconstruction, I was fortunate enough to be a student in theologian and pastor Brad Jersak's classes at WTC. Through his teaching, I discovered a hidden doctrinal gem. In his lectures and his book, *A More Christlike God*, Brad unpacks an understanding of salvation that arguably is very like the beautiful hidden panelling in our home. It is an old and more beautiful view of the saving work of Jesus that has been covered over by other (more modern) explanations.[33]

---

[33] Bradley Jersak, *A More Christlike God: A More Beautiful Gospel* (Plain Truth Ministries, Pasadena, 2015).

Saved from what?

'Salvation' is an often-misunderstood word, but essentially it means to be rescued from harm. Christians believe that Jesus is the saviour not just of each one of us but also of the world. If this is the case, then it begs the question, what harm is Jesus rescuing us from? I've been a Christian for a long time but, to be honest, before our winter season I could not have given you an answer to this question.

I grew up with a view of salvation that treated it much like a transaction, almost a court proceeding. I was the guilty one who deserved punishment, and God was the judge. At the last minute in my court case, in walked Jesus, and He saved me by taking the penalty for my wrongdoing. This means that God can forgive me, I am reconciled to Him and get to go to heaven when I die. Following this through to its logical conclusion, in this model of salvation, Jesus saves me from God.

In this model of salvation, God's justice is retributive; for justice to be done, someone needs to be punished. Jesus takes our punishment; He takes the consequence of our wrongdoing. The consequence is death. What's more, God can't forgive us until justice is done. Furthermore, this explanation reduces the saving work of Jesus to the cross – to Good Friday. I appreciate that this is oversimplifying and caricaturing it, but this is the essence of what I believed.

I will always remember the day I sat in Brad's doctrine class as he unpacked 'The Gospel in Chairs'.[34] As I listened to Brad talk about how God loves us, isn't angry with us, has always been for us and always will be, I felt as though a massive weight was being lifted off my shoulders.

The gospel is not about a wrathful, vengeful God who, in order to forgive us and reconcile Himself to us, punishes His

---

[34] To see Brad do this himself and explain it far better than I could, see 'Brad Jersak – The Gospel In Chairs',
https://www.youtube.com/watch?v=D0BUFR9wSko (accessed 6th November 2020).

Son in our place. The word 'gospel' means 'good news', and this is decidedly not good news. Salvation is not about Jesus rescuing us from the Father. No, the gospel is about a loving Father who is and has always been turned towards us. He is the loving Father that Jesus talks about in the story of the Prodigal Son (Luke 15:11-32). A Father who is always scanning the horizon waiting for us to return home. When He sees us, what does He do? He doesn't stand there with a wagging finger reminding us of all we have done wrong. Quite the opposite: He runs towards us, embraces us and celebrates that we have come home.

God knows that we don't need further punishment for our sins, as American philosopher Elbert Hubbard points out: 'We are punished by our sins not for them.'[35] Just think about the effects of human brokenness in terms of war, murder, drug and alcohol addiction, family breakdown and climate change, to name a few. The consequences of sin in terms of the suffering it inflicts on us, on those around us and on the natural world are enough.

What about justice?

When I talk about this with people, one of their objections is that God is a God of justice; therefore, there must be punishment for wrongdoing (for sin). I track with them through the first part – yes, I firmly believe in the justice of God – but what exactly is sin? Is it merely lawbreaking? Or is it more profound than that? Could it be something fundamentally wrong with human nature that needs to be healed? If it is the latter, then punishment is not going to bring about justice, it's not going to bring change and healing. I believe that God's justice is all about freeing us and healing our brokenness, and

---

[35] Elbert Hubbard quoted in Christopher L Heuertz, *The Sacred Enneagram: Finding your Unique Path to Spiritual Growth* (Zondervan, Grand Rapids, 2017), p77.

reconciling us to Him, to ourselves, and to others. Rather than being retributive, it's restorative.

Think about it in terms of the criminal justice system; we believe that justice is done when someone is punished for their crime. For example, when a murderer is imprisoned, we often hear people say, 'Justice has been done.' But punishment doesn't solve the problem. It doesn't heal the brokenness of the person who committed the crime. More often than not, it just creates a vicious cycle of brokenness and bitterness where, upon release from prison, the person goes on to commit more crime. What's more, punishment doesn't free the victims of crime either.

Within the criminal justice system there is mounting evidence that what is needed to create lasting change, both for those committing crimes and for the victims, is restorative justice.[36] Here, both parties are given the opportunity to meet. Victims can talk about how the crime has affected them and the perpetrators of the crime talk about what led them to it and are given an opportunity to ask for forgiveness. Restorative justice reconciles people to each other, which leads to freedom for both parties. Research has demonstrated that restorative justice is a more effective form of justice in terms of creating real and lasting change.[37] If this is the case in the criminal justice system, might God have got there first in terms of what true justice looks like?

When seen through this lens of healing and restoration, we can see that the gospel encompasses the whole of Jesus' life, not merely His death. Yes, salvation is about forgiveness of sins, but it is so much than just this; it is about healing us and the world.

---

[36] For a report on restorative justice within the criminal justice system, see Lawrence W Sherman and Heather Strang, 'Restorative justice: The Evidence' (The Smith Institute, London, 2007),
http://www.iirp.edu/pdf/RJ_full_report.pdf (accessed 6th November 2020).

[37] For a beautiful portrayal of the power of restorative justice I highly recommend you watch the 2013 film *The Railway Man*.

Theologian Richard Foster writes, 'We are, to be sure, reconciled to God by Jesus' death, but even more, we are "saved" by his life.'[38]

Jesus says in John's Gospel that anyone who has seen Him has seen the Father (John 14:9). Through His life, death and resurrection, Jesus shows us a Father who loves us, who is always turned towards us, always ready to forgive and heal us. More than this, Jesus' death shows us the depth of this love, that there is nothing God wouldn't do to rescue and heal us and that there is nowhere that His love does not extend to; not even death can conquer it. The apostle Paul says:

> For I am convinced that neither death, nor life, nor angels, nor rulers, nor things present, nor things to come, nor powers, nor height, nor depth, nor anything else in all creation, will be able to separate us from the love of God in Christ Jesus our Lord.
> *Romans 8:38-39*

This is the truth that we need to hear in the midst of our pain: that God is not an angry, distant God but a Father who loves us passionately and is always with us, and that there is no situation in life that can separate us from His love. Nothing that happens to us – the loss of a child or loved one, a terminal diagnosis, a life-changing accident, the loss of a job or home, or even the wrong choices we make in life – can separate us from God's love.

Collecting tears

The life of Jesus also shows us the co-suffering nature of God's love for us. Rather than distancing Himself from our pain and

---

[38] Richard Foster, *Streams of Living Water: Celebrating the Great Traditions of Christian Faith* (Hodder & Stoughton, London, 2017), p3.

suffering, in Jesus we have a God who gets down into the mess with us. He suffers with and alongside us. Eugene Peterson's Message paraphrase puts it this way: 'The Word became flesh and blood, and moved into the neighborhood' (John 1:14, *The Message*).

Jesus reveals a God of compassion. The word 'compassion' originates from two Latin words: *com*, meaning 'with or together', and *pati,* which means 'to suffer'. Compassion means 'to suffer with'. We see this throughout the life of Jesus: He revealed a co-suffering God, a God who has wholly entered into all the brokenness that we go through, even enduring the suffering and torture of death on a cross.

I think one of the stories that powerfully demonstrates the co-suffering love of Jesus is the death and resurrection of Lazarus (John 11:1-46). When Jesus arrives at Lazarus' tomb, we are told that He weeps. Why does Jesus cry when it seems so evident in the narrative leading up to this verse that He knows He is going to raise Lazarus from the dead? While some theologians have found it difficult to believe, I think the tears that Jesus sheds are a demonstration of the truth that Jesus is fully human. Here we have Jesus fully entering into the human experience of grief; this is compassion in action. Jesus is suffering with Martha and Mary, the sisters of Lazarus, even though He knows what is about to happen.[39]

I find it amazingly powerful and comforting to think that when I weep over all that we have lost, Jesus weeps with me. He sits in the darkness with me and suffers with me; He doesn't rush me on to the end of the story, even though He knows the ending.

One of the verses that I had stuck on my fridge after Libby died is from Psalm 56, where King David says:

---

[39] For more on this see F F Bruce, *The Gospel of John: A Verse-by-Verse Exposition* (Kingsley Books, Nashville, 2018, accessed from Scribd (www.scribd.com)), pp409-410.

> You keep track of all my sorrows.
> You have collected all my tears in your bottle.
> You have recorded each one in your book.
> *Psalm 56:8 (NLT)*

I love the intimacy and care to which these words allude. As we cry, not one of our tears is missed by our loving heavenly Father; He sees them all. I also love the idea that the tears we cry are so precious to God that rather than just letting them fall, He collects them.

Powerful as it might be to know that God loves us, is for us and suffers with us, it means little if we can't incarnate this truth in our lives. We might know all of this in terms of 'head' knowledge, but how do we transfer it to our hearts so that we actually experience God's love? It is to this question that I want us to turn next.

Walk it out

- How has the gospel been explained to you in the past?

- What parts of this chapter do you find encouraging? What are the challenges for you?

- You might like to spend some time reflecting on the story of the lost son found in Luke 15:11-32. Picture yourself in this story. How does it feel to know that God is a loving Father who is always scanning the horizon, waiting for you to come home?

A new pillar

I have calmed and quieted my soul,

like a weaned child with its mother;

my soul is like the weaned child that is with me.

Psalm 131:2

Before renovating our house, the ceiling above the window in our living room was, to put it mildly, rather wonky and by no means flat. While we tried to convince ourselves that this was just a charming 'feature' of a sixteenth-century home, both Jon and I knew that this was highly unlikely and that the bumpy nature of the ceiling probably hid a significant structural issue. As it turned out, this was precisely the case. When the builders stripped the plaster of the ceiling back, they found that the wooden joists had been eaten away by some nasty bug. Rather than running to the wall above the window, they stopped several inches short. Fortunately for us, we had not been living in the part of the house directly above the sitting room. Had we put any furniture up there, there is a strong possibility that at some point it would have arrived rather unceremoniously in our sitting room!

The solution to this problem was, of course, to put new joists in to support the floor above. We also put a new oak pillar in the middle of our living room to support the main beam in the ceiling. Without making these changes, the rooms upstairs would have been unsafe and therefore unusable.

In the same way that stripping back our ceiling revealed the true scale of our problem, when my faith was stripped back by loss, I realised that not only were the supports of my faith rotten, but I was also missing a central pillar. It was at this time, when the structural shortcomings of my faith were revealed, I was introduced to the contemplative stream of Christian spirituality.

As I have said, I grew up with a faith that was all about 'doing for God'; it was all about being busy. In stark contrast to this, the contemplative tradition is about stopping, about ceasing our doing and instead allowing ourselves to rest in God's love for us. As Richard Foster articulates so beautifully, the contemplative tradition is 'always calling us back to our beginnings, always forcing us to the root, always reminding us of our foundations'.[40] This has been my experience. It was only after my faith was stripped back by pain and suffering that I discovered this stream of faith, and it was as though God had taken me right back to the foundations.

Just like our home, rather than trying to paper over the cracks, as it were, God, as the divine builder, knew that I needed to strip my faith right back to the foundations. Only by doing this, by focusing on God's love for me, would I experience the intimacy of His presence, and it would be this sense of His loving presence with me that would sustain and strengthen me to face and walk on through winter.

When Libby died, I needed to root myself in God's love for me; this was the foundation that God would use to restore and rebuild the home that was my faith. Just like the new pillar in our living room, contemplative spirituality was to become a new source of strength that would allow me to face and journey through the cold, dark, stormy and wet winter.

---

[40] Richard Foster, *Streams of Living Water*, p51.

Contemplative spirituality is not about doing; it's about being. It's about stopping all the activity and allowing ourselves to be with our loving heavenly Father, to abide in that place. As Richard Foster says, 'The contemplative life is the steady gaze of the soul upon the God who loves us.'[41] We don't come to God because we need something from Him. The former Archbishop of Canterbury Rowan Williams has said that contemplating God means 'to look to God without regard to my own instant satisfaction'.[42] In the verse from Psalm 131 which I quoted at the beginning of this chapter, King David says he is like a weaned child with its mother. A weaned child is not looking to its mother for milk. It is not needy in that way. Instead, the child comes simply to be in its mother's presence and held in her loving embrace.

Contemplative spirituality prioritises practices such as silence, stillness, solitude, and centring prayer as ways to become more aware of God's loving presence in the whole of our lives. Christian mystics, far from being weird, slightly hippy, other-worldly people, are simply those who prize intimacy with God above everything else.

Contemplative spirituality doesn't deny the importance of action; quite the opposite: it leads us to action rather than reaction. Why? Because contemplative practices help us to stay present to God and His love, to abide in His love and to live from this place.[43] Abiding in God's love will change our perspective on the world and hence how we act in it. This is summed up in God's famous words at the end of Psalm 46: 'Be still, and know that I am God!' These words come at the end of a psalm all about not being afraid when all we see around us is chaos, nations raging, the earth giving way. The temptation when the world seems to be falling apart on either a personal or

---

[41] Richard Foster, *Streams of Living Water*, p49.
[42] Rowan Williams, quoted in Chris E W Green, *Surprised by God*, p11.
[43] If this is something you are interested in, I thoroughly recommend Brian Draper's beautiful book, *Soulfulness: Deepening the Mindful Life* (Hodder & Stoughton, London, 2016).

a global scale is to rush to action. Amid the chaos, contemplative spirituality calls us to 'be still' and, as a result of being still, to realise again who God is and who we are in Him. It is from this place of stillness, security and intimacy that He gives us our unique commission in response to the brokenness of the world.

This ability to abide in God's love is essential as we journey through winter. Rather than reacting to our circumstances and seeing them as a problem to solve, it allows us to cultivate intimacy with God and an awareness of His loving presence right in the middle of our pain. In contemplative spirituality, suffering and pain are not something to be fixed but something to be faced and journeyed through with God. They are a place where we can experience intimacy with Him.

Walk it out

- What are the ways that you have been busy doing? For example, how are you busy trying to fix your situation or to avoid it? How are you busy doing for God? How do you feel about stopping to be still and just be with God?

- Try taking some time each day to sit with Jesus in silence and solitude. This doesn't have to be long – start with five minutes each day. You might like to picture yourself meeting Jesus in a favourite place. For me this is at a beach I love. Picture yourself sitting with Jesus, and simply enjoy just being with Him. When you feel ready ask Him, 'What do you to say to me today?'

- Spend some time reflecting on Psalm 131. Picture yourself as a child in your heavenly Father's arms. Allow yourself just to spend time in His loving embrace without asking anything of Him. Simply enjoy being with Him.

Who am I?

It's in Christ that we find out who we are and what we are living for.

Ephesians 1:11 (*The Message*)

I will always vividly remember the full force of the 'Who am I?' question hitting me as I sat in the bereavement flat at the hospital the day after Libby had been born. As well as being plunged into the darkness of grief, when I lost Libby, I also lost myself.

I had dealt with what I thought was an 'identity crisis' when I finished work to go on maternity leave. I hadn't realised how tightly I had tied my identity to the job I did. To be honest, rather than addressing this, I simply chose to focus on the fact that I was about to become a mother, and that gave me a new sense of identity and purpose. But I had carried a baby and given birth to her only to have to let her go immediately. I carried Libby for nine months but only got to hold her for two days. This, of course, is not even to mention the five other babies that I carried but never got to hold.

My desperate prayer the day after Libby died went something like this: 'Lord, I have no job, no baby to look after... no clue what I do now and absolutely no idea who I am. I need You to show me.'

The three lies of identity

I know that I am not unusual in that a season of loss and trauma led me to question who I am. Speaker and author Sheridan Voysey wrote an excellent book on his pilgrimage with this question as a result of his journey through childlessness.[44] To use the metaphor of our home renovation, I think seasons of loss cause us to question our identity because they reveal the rotten joists we have been using to support it.

In my pilgrimage with the question of personal identity, I have found the teachings of Henri Nouwen, a Roman Catholic priest, academic and pastor at L'Arche, to be hugely insightful and healing.[45] Nouwen taught that there are essentially three lies that we believe about who we are: 'I am what I do,' 'I am what others say about me,' and, 'I am what I have.' Let's unpack these a little bit.

I am what I do

In our society of productivity and achievement, the lie that we are what we do is a big one. Think about when we meet new people: what is one of the first questions we ask someone in our attempts to get to know them? 'What do you do?'

What we do could be our paid work: plumber, doctor, builder, teacher, writer, scientist, small business owner – there are too many different ones to name. Or we might be a stay-at-home parent (this is, in my opinion, the most demanding job

[44] Sheridan Voysey, *The Making of Us: Who We Can Become When Life Doesn't Go as Planned* (Thomas Nelson, Nashville, 2019).
[45] For more on this I would recommend reading the following: Henri J M Nouwen with Michael J Christensen and Rebecca J Laird, *Spiritual Direction: Wisdom for the Long Walk of Faith* (HarperCollins, New York, 2006), particularly the chapter entitled 'Who Am I?'; and Henri J M Nouwen, *Life of the Beloved: Spiritual Living in a Secular World* (Crossroad Publishing Company, New York, 2002, accessed from Scribd (www.scribd.com)).

going!), or perhaps we're studying at school or university, or we volunteer for a local charity or church.

Or it could be what we have done in the past, being able to point to past achievements and say, 'Look what I did.' Perhaps in our youth we were a professional sportsperson, for example. Or maybe we're now retired but we had a very successful career and led a major organisation.

Equally, we might define ourselves by what we haven't been able to do. In my work with WTC, I regularly came across people who told me that they weren't up to studying with us because they hadn't done well at school. I loved seeing these people, as they studied with WTC, realise they had been believing a lie. Or perhaps we haven't been able to realise a long-held dream when it comes to work. Maybe for financial reasons we feel 'stuck' in a job that pays the bills but is not life-giving.

As well as the things we do for work, 'I am what I do' applies to our behaviour. When we do things well – for example, we're loving and kind to our family and friends, we're successful at work or we stick to our diet or exercise regime – we feel good about ourselves. But what happens when we're not doing so well? When I was teaching on this topic, in response to how we apply 'I am what I do' to our lives, someone once said, 'I am impatient with my children.' I can definitely relate to this! I spend a lot of my time beating myself up for not being a better parent, for losing my temper with Charlie. How many of us parents have put children to bed at night, silently vowing to do better tomorrow?

It could be that we've tried something in the past, maybe a business venture that didn't work out. Or we didn't pass the required exams for a professional qualification, or perhaps we started a degree but didn't finish it. In these circumstances, it's so easy to brand ourselves as a failure because of what we couldn't do.

It could also be something that was done to us that defines our sense of identity. It is all too tragically common for victims of child abuse to spend their lives being defined by the awful things that someone else did to them.

Defining ourselves by the things we can't do or by the worst things we do, have done or have had done to us, leads to shame. It brings a sense that at the core I'm not a good person, which leads us to hide from others out of fear that if they were to see what we think is the 'real me' we would be rejected and judged.

Why is 'I am what I do' such an easy lie for us to believe? I think it's because busyness has become the way we prove to others that we are significant. If I'm busy, I must be important. Sadly, in my experience, many Christians are often no better when it comes to believing this lie; we just get busy 'doing' for God.

Circling back to the scenario of encountering new people, after Libby died, the 'What do you do?' question was one of the reasons I dreaded meeting new people. I so hated it that I have given a lot of thought over the years to how I can avoid asking this question of others. In this regard, my spiritual director gave me some excellent advice. She told me that, instead of asking, 'What do you do?' when she meets new people, she says, 'Tell me something of your story.' I have now started doing this, and I love it. People tell me really fascinating things about themselves and their life stories. I'd encourage you to give it a go next time you meet someone new.

I am what others say about me

Personally, this is a big one for me. I know I spend a lot of my life worrying about what other people think of me. At its heart, this is about the need to be approved of, accepted and loved by others. This need can manifest itself in every area of our lives.

In our work, the need for the praise and approval of those we work with can mean we work long hours and have an inability to say no to people. Or it could be in our parenting and close relationships, where we work hard to be affirmed by others and to be told that we are a good parent, friend or family member. It could also be about our appearance and only feeling

OK about ourselves when people say good things about how we look, such as when someone compliments us on what we are wearing, a new haircut, the fact that we have lost weight or how the hours at the gym are paying off in terms of muscle mass and strength. On the flip side of this, when someone criticises or rejects us, it can be devastating as it hits the core of how we define our identity.

Continually looking for the approval and admiration of others leads to a life of people pleasing, of trying to keep everyone happy so that they will accept and affirm us. Living this way is exhausting. We have to keep performing to feel accepted by others and therefore to feel good about who we are. For me, this means I spend my life second-guessing what others are thinking. I struggle to make decisions out of fear of what other people might think. I also know that I am prone to taking things on, to saying yes to people and projects that I really shouldn't, simply to gain (or keep) their approval and admiration. This means I often end up overstretched and with limited resources for the things that really matter.

Like 'I am what I do', 'I am what others say about me' can apply not only to what people currently say about us but also to what people have said in the past. We might have been told as a child that we weren't particularly clever, or that we weren't as attractive as a sibling or a friend. Worse still, we may have been abused and had awful lies spoken over us about being a bad person who deserved the treatment we were getting. I don't believe it's an understatement to say that these things others say over us are curses: they have the power to affect our sense of identity and, as a result, our behaviour.

Or it might have been that others regularly praised us because we excelled academically, in a sport or musically. Building our sense of self on what others say about us means that we will feel compelled to keep performing, to keep excelling, in order to be admired and affirmed by others. I know from personal experience this is a heavy burden to carry, often leading to a fear of disappointing others if we don't live up to their expectations (real or imagined).

I am what I have

In the consumer society we live in, it's easy to see this lie in operation. We can tie our identity up in all the stuff we have – for example, some of us work hard so that we can buy our dream car or home. For others of us, it's about having fashionable clothes or the latest gadgets.

'I am what I have' is not just about our possessions; it can be about having been to the right school and university – having received a 'good education'. Or it can be about physical appearance. For a woman, having a perfectly toned and slim body; for a man having a 'six-pack'.

Or what about our relationships? As well as defining ourselves by the job we do, we can define ourselves by our role as mother, father, daughter, son, sibling or friend. Being popular, having a wide network of friends, is often used as another marker of success in our world.

Just like with the other two lies, the flip side of 'I am what I have' – 'I am what I don't have' – can define our sense of identity too. When we were going through our winter season, it was a fight for me not to define myself by what I didn't have – children. For you, it might be about not having a partner or feeling like you don't have enough friends. Or it could be about your possessions, a sense that you don't have the perfect house, enough clothes, gadgets or whatever is your 'thing'.

The roller coaster

Latterly, Nouwen added two more lies to his original three: 'I am nothing more than my worst moment' and 'I am nothing more than my best moment'. It is very easy to reduce our lives to the worst things we have done, or that others have said about us, or what we don't have, and to define ourselves based on this.

The opposite is also true: that we can root our identity in the best things we've done, or possess, or that others have said about us.

The problem with believing any one of these five lies is that it puts us on a roller coaster where one minute we can be on top of the world – when we do great things, people are effusive in their praise of us, or we finally acquire our 'forever' home or marry the person of our dreams. But what happens when life falls apart when we fail or lose a job? Or people criticise us? Or our marriage falls apart? Or we lose our health? Or in my case when my babies died? And what about the times of significant transition in life like when children leave home, we move to a new area or we retire. Who are we then?

The coronavirus crisis raised so many questions of identity. Millions were furloughed from work with no idea when or if they would be returning. Businesses that before the crisis were doing well found themselves teetering on the edge of collapse. Working parents tried desperately to juggle working from home with homeschooling children. I know in my case this left me feeling like I wasn't doing any of it well. Or maybe we were told by the government that because of a medical condition, we were vulnerable and so were advised not to leave our home for weeks on end.

Look up

As well as leaving us on a roller coaster of highs and lows, another danger of believing these lies of identity is that it leads to constant comparison with others. Australian pastor and author Mark Sayers says that our culture defines identity by looking horizontally not vertically.[46] We look to those around us, to the external world, to give us a sense of identity. Looking around, not up, means we measure ourselves relative to other

[46] Mark Sayers, *The Vertical Self: How Biblical Faith Can Help Us Discover Who We Are in an Age of Self Obsession* (Thomas Nelson, Nashville, 2010).

people, which leads us into a battle with the voice of our inner critic, the voice that tells us that we are not doing enough, people don't like us enough or we don't have enough: basically that we are not enough. This endless comparison is something that I want to come back to in a later chapter.

At the heart of the issue of personal identity are the human needs to be loved, to belong, to feel significant and to feel that our life has meaning and purpose. These needs are not wrong; it's just that we are looking in the wrong places to meet them. We all have a hole in our soul, and we attempt to fill it with the things of this world. We look to the horizontal to give us identity when, in truth, this hole can only be filled by looking vertically, to God. Rather than looking out, we need to look in and up. We need to know who we are in our inmost being and allow this knowledge to flow out into our doing. It's our being that should define our doing. So often we get this the wrong way around and attempt to define our being by our doing.

Humanity rebooted

So what is the Christian response to the 'Who am I?' question? If I am not what I do, or what others say about me, or what I have, who am I? Biblically, there are several ways to answer this question. Humanity, we are told in Genesis 1:26-27, is made in the image of God. There is so much more to what this term means than I can unpack here,[47] but one of the connotations of being made in the image of God is that we are children of God. In the same way that biological children are made in the image of their parents, we are made in God's image. As children of God, the Bible affirms that we are deeply and intimately known by Him.

---

[47] If this is a topic that interests you, I highly recommend J Richard Middleton's book, *The Liberating Image: The Imago Dei in Genesis 1* (Brazos Press, Grand Rapids, 2005).

Tragically, the Fall fractured human identity. As the theologian Brian Rosner articulates, 'The serpent's lies were designed to undermine Adam and Eve's confidence in God and to tempt them to find their identity independently of him.'[48] However, the biblical story is a story of redemption, and at the heart of this is the redemption and restoration of humanity to their true God-given identity as beloved sons and daughters, made in His image and known by Him.

We see this supremely in Jesus, who came to restore and redeem all that we lost in the Garden of Eden; this includes the restoration of humanity's true identity. He modelled for us how to live a truly human life. Through His life, death and resurrection, He 'rebooted' humanity. It is in Jesus that we find new and real life. Jesus came so that we might 'have life, and have it abundantly' (John 10:10). It is through faith in Jesus that we are adopted back into the family of God and restored to our true God-given identity. For this reason, the apostle Paul repeatedly talks about being 'in Christ'. Just as a branch of a tree is united with the trunk, so we are united with Jesus. Paul goes so far as to say that when we come to faith, our old selves are crucified with Christ so that it is no longer we who live, but Christ who lives in us (Galatians 2:20). By faith in Jesus, we become new people, no longer tied to Adam but united to Jesus. As a result, our old life is gone, and our new one begins (see 2 Corinthians 5:17).

Beloved

Through Jesus, we are adopted back into God's family as His beloved sons and daughters. As I walked through winter, this was the most important thing I needed to know: that I am a beloved child of God. Or as spiritual director and psychologist David Benner says, 'The fact that I am deeply loved by God is

---

[48] Brian S Rosner, *Known by God: A Biblical Theology of Personal Identity* (Zondervan, Grand Rapids, 2017), pp86-87.

the core of my identity, what I know about myself with most confidence.'[49] The Christian faith teaches us that it is in God that our needs for love, belonging and significance are truly and fully met.

If you have been a Christian for any length of time, it's unlikely that this statement is new to you. I think we all know the truth of it in our heads, but transferring it to our hearts is a different matter. The problem is that it's only when something becomes 'heart knowledge' that we begin to live from that place. As Nouwen articulated, we need to incarnate the truth of our belovedness. We need to know it not just in our heads; we need to live it out – to enflesh it.[50]

To do this, we need to absolutely know that we don't have to (and cannot) earn the Father's love, affirmation and acceptance. They are unconditional. I think we all struggle with the unconditional nature of God's love for us. Very few of us will have experienced truly unconditional love from those around us. It's all too easy to allow our human experience of love to colour our view of God's love, to believe the lie that says I have to do spectacular things or be a better person for God to love me.

Here, it is beneficial to turn to the Gospel accounts of Jesus' baptism to counter this lie (Matthew 3:13-17; Mark 1:9-11; Luke 3:21-22). I think it's fascinating that three of the four Gospels tell this story; the repetition is important. In each account we are told that as Jesus came up out of the water, heaven was opened, the Spirit of God descended on Jesus and a voice from heaven was heard saying, 'This is my Son, the Beloved; with whom I am well pleased.' Or as *The Message* paraphrase says, 'This is my Son, chosen and marked by my love, delight of my life' (Matthew 3:17). Crucially, this affirmation of the Son by the Father comes before Jesus starts His public ministry. This is

---

[49] David G Benner, *Surrender to Love: Discovering the Heart of Christian Spirituality* (InterVarsity Press, Downers Grove, 2015), p31.
[50] Henri J M Nouwen, *Life of the Beloved*, p29.

before He does any of the spectacular stuff like walking on water, healing sick people or raising the dead. This is the Father affirming His son Jesus and declaring His love for Him not for what He can do, or for what others say about Him or for what He has, but simply for who He is.

Moreover, this assurance of the Father's love and delight, this grounding of Jesus' identity as the beloved Son, comes just before He is then sent by the Spirit into the wilderness to be tempted by the devil. Interestingly, in two of the three temptations, the devil starts with, 'If you are the Son of God ...' (Matthew 4:1-11; Luke 4:1-12). This is what the enemy has done to humanity from the beginning: attempted to sow a seed of doubt about our God-given identity.

Recently I was preparing a talk based on this, and I was trying to find funny/inspiring quotes about identity online (I wasted far too much time on this!). Several of the quotes or images talked about identity theft in terms of bank fraud. At the time, I ignored them all, but as I wrote my talk, I realised that the devil is the perpetrator of the ultimate identity theft. He wants to rob the whole of humanity of our God-given identity. The truth is that the words spoken over Jesus at His baptism are the same words that God the Father speaks over us.

You may be reading this and thinking, yes, but Jesus was perfect, and I'm not. Maybe we feel that we are so broken and have done so much wrong in our lives that we need to 'sort ourselves out' in some way before God will love us. Personally, I find it much easier to believe that God loves other people unconditionally but not me, because I know the 'real me', the parts that I don't let others see. But the truth is that we are all broken; none of us has it 'all together'. More than this, God knows us; He sees all of us – the good the bad and the ugly! He knit us together in our mothers' wombs (Psalm 139:13). Nothing we have done, are doing or will do comes as a surprise to God, and it certainly doesn't change His love for us.

I don't want you to misunderstand me. There is a simplicity to this message, but getting to the point where we incarnate it, where we live from the truth of it, is not simple. I know, from personal experience, that the negative and self-rejecting thought patterns are like well-worn ruts that take time and effort to get out of. But it is possible to live more fully from this place. The way through to the truth, to being able to live from this place of knowing we are the beloved, is through surrender. We need to stop coming up with ifs and buts, to stop fighting and let go, and surrender to the unconditional love of the Father.

Stepping into the river

As I finish this chapter, I want to address one of the objections that I have beaten myself up with on my journey inwards to discover my true, God-given identity. It is the lie that focusing on this issue of identity is in some way self-absorbed – narcissistic, if you like; a feeling that I'm just being influenced by the culture in which I live, which is arguably the most self-obsessed society ever. I was listening to a radio programme the other day that talked about the fact that until the nineteenth century, the term 'self-fulfilment' didn't exist. Now it's everywhere and seems to be the goal of life. Just think about the overwhelming number of 'self-help' books that are available.

Our culture tells people that they can be anything they want to be. In our quest for greater personal freedom, we have lauded choice as the answer to all our problems. But we are now learning that, rather than freeing us, too much choice leads to anxiety. We are afraid of making the wrong choice. As a trivial example, I have wasted hours of my life on the internet just trying to buy something simple, such as printer paper, and being bombarded with too many different options. I then spend too much time reading all the reviews in an attempt not to make the wrong choice when, at the end of the day, it's just printer paper.

In his book *Known by God*, Brian Rosner talks about the difference between modern and traditional societies. He explains that traditional societies had/have far less choice when it comes to the big questions of life: where we will live, what we will do, who we will marry. Rosner goes on to quote Polish sociologist Zygmunt Bauman, who likens traditional societies to rivers and modern ones to oceans. He explains that rivers have a direction, a flow, to them, whereas oceans have no direction. What's more, there is far more chance of getting lost or drowning in an ocean.[51] I believe this is precisely what we see in our culture. People are drowning in an ocean of choice when it comes to questions of identity. All this choice leads to anxiety, restlessness, dissatisfaction and 'FOMO' – the fear of missing out.

Rather than feeling fulfilled and free, all our culture's attention on being whoever we want to be, doing whatever we want to do, with whomever we want, and acquiring whatever makes us happy, has bound us in tighter bondage to the lies of identity, leaving us more confused about who we really are.

Coming back to my concern that, as a Christian, too much focus on personal identity is not a good thing, I would argue that the Christian response to the 'Who am I?' question frees us from self-absorption. It helps us 'get ourselves out of the way', if you like. Why? Because when we ground ourselves in the love of God, we are not looking to external things or to other people to shore up a fragile sense of identity. We are free to love and serve others out of the overflow of the perfect and unconditional love we receive from our heavenly Father.

The image of a river that gives life is used repeatedly in the Bible. For example, in the book of the prophet Ezekiel there is a beautiful passage where Ezekiel has a vision of the restored Temple from which a river flows. This river gives life to 'swarms of living creatures' and to a great number of trees (Ezekiel 47:1-12, NIVUK). As the river flows from the Temple, it gets deeper and deeper, until eventually Ezekiel finds himself swimming in it. Rather than leaving us drowning in an ocean of choice, Jesus' invitation to each of us is to step into the river of God's love

---

[51] Brian S Rosner, *Known by God*, pp25-26.

for us. Crucially, it's in the river of God's love that we will find direction, meaning and purpose for our lives.

Walk it out

- Spend some time with the three lies of identity. Ask God through His Spirit to reveal the areas in your life where you believe any one or a combination of these lies. Journal your thoughts and anything that God says to you.

- Reflect on Matthew's account of Jesus' baptism (Matthew 3:13-17). Picture yourself in the story. You may want to personalise God the Father's words, 'This is my Son, the Beloved, with whom I am well pleased,' with your name.

- You might like to try practising centring prayer. Start with five minutes each day in silence and solitude. When your mind wanders (which it will), bring yourself back to the presence of God with the word 'Beloved'.

What's the point?

What joy for those whose strength comes from the LORD ...

When they walk through the Valley of Weeping,

it will become a place of refreshing springs.

Psalm 84:5-6 (NLT)

One of the things that often accompanies a winter season is a sense of waste. Perhaps we put our heart and soul into building a career or a business only to see it wiped away in the wake of a recession or the coronavirus pandemic. Or maybe we invested time, energy and effort in a marriage or relationship that has fallen apart. In the wake of the loss, we find ourselves questioning what the point of it all was, all the time, effort and work. And, more significantly, perhaps asking, 'How do I find purpose in life again after I have seen everything that I've worked for go up in flames?'

When Libby died, I struggled with an enormous sense of waste that her death brought with it. I had put a massive amount of energy – physical, emotional and spiritual – into growing my beautiful baby girl, only to see it all be for nothing. There was so much potential carried in her, and it felt like none of it would ever be realised. As the 'Who am I?' question swirled around in my head, I also struggled to know what the purpose of my life now was, let alone attempt to find any meaning in a world that seemed random and capricious.

Catastrophic loss creates chaos; I often describe Libby's death as being akin to a bomb going off in my life, with all the resulting chaos that a bomb brings. Where once life might have felt ordered and controlled, it's now chaotic and out of control. For many of us, when this happens, it's natural to want to return to normal, to get things back to the way they were as quickly as possible. We want to restore our sense of order and control. But the painful truth is that control is only ever a thin veneer, and the normal you once knew no longer exists; it has been lost along with everything else.

Forest bathing

I love the Japanese practice of *shinrin-yoku*, or 'forest bathing'. Forest bathing is not a brisk walk through the woods with your dog or a friend. Gary Evans, founder of The Forest Bathing Institute in the UK, says, 'Forest bathing is mindful time spent under the canopy of trees for health and wellbeing purposes.'[52] It's about taking time to be present to our surroundings, to wander through and wonder at the natural beauty of woodlands.

Evidence is now building that this practice of taking time to walk through woods can have beneficial effects on our health, such as lowering blood pressure, reducing the stress hormone cortisol and improving concentration and memory. Recently, the Woodland Trust in the UK suggested that, because of its potential benefits, forest bathing should be part of a range of measures known as 'social prescribing'. These are activities known to improve well-being, such as regular exercise, volunteering, cooking or gardening.[53]

---

[52] Gary Evans quoted in Harriet Sherwood, 'Getting back to nature: how forest bathing can make us feel better', *The Guardian*, 8 June 2019, https://www.theguardian.com/environment/2019/jun/08/forest-bathing-japanese-practice-in-west-wellbeing (accessed 6th November 2020).
[53] Harriet Sherwood, 'Getting back to nature: how forest bathing can make us feel better'.

I have experienced the benefits of regular 'forest bathing'. There is a beech wood near me that I love to walk through. I find it a calming place to be: from the moment I set foot in the woodland, I feel my pace and my pulse slow down. I feel myself breathe more deeply and slowly. For me, it is a 'thin place', where the divide between earth and heaven recedes a little. It is somewhere I often go if I want to experience God and hear Him speak.

During one of my walks through these woods, I felt God draw my attention to the woodland floor. Like any woodland, it was covered in dead and decomposing matter – last year's leaves, old bits of bark, and so on. I felt God remind me of something I had learnt in my biology lessons (and long since forgotten): in nature, nothing is ever lost; it is simply recycled. What's more, the cycling of matter is fundamental to the creation of new life. When leaves fall to the woodland floor, a process of decomposition is initiated. In this process, detritivores such as worms, woodlice, decomposing bacteria and fungi break down the leaves to recycle the nutrients contained within them. Death in one organism brings life in another. This is the way it works in nature – nothing is ever wasted.

In the woodland that day, as I looked down at all the decomposing natural material, I felt God say to me that, in the same way that nature never wastes anything, He never wastes any of the experiences that we walk through. In His hands, the greatest losses of our lives can be restored and redeemed; new life can come from death.

Not only is death necessary for new life, but chaos in nature, rather than being something to be feared, is the crucible of creativity. Author and leadership expert Margaret Wheatley articulates:

> Disorder can be a source of new order ... growth
> appears from disequilibrium, not balance. The things
> we fear most ... disruptions, confusions, chaos –

need not be interpreted as signs that we are about to be destroyed. Instead, these conditions are necessary to awaken creativity.[54]

As I write, in the midst of the coronavirus pandemic, the thought that the chaos, rather than leading to destruction, can instead be the catalyst for new life, that it can birth new ways of being and doing, gives me great hope. Who knows what creative solutions will come out of this crisis? Not only in the way we treat and prevent the disease itself but in other areas of life, such as the climate emergency, how we educate our children, where we buy our food from, how and where we work.

The message of the Bible is that God can and does bring new life out of death. As Joseph says to his brothers when they are finally reunited in the famous biblical story, 'Even though you intended to do harm to me, God intended it for good, in order to preserve a numerous people, as he is doing today' (Genesis 50:20). We see this supremely in Jesus: His death released new life for the whole of creation.

This truth does not negate all the awful things that come with a winter season; it does not belittle the losses. We need to be real about all the pain and heartache that come with loss, something we will look at when we turn to 'brave the elements' of winter seasons.

I also want to make it very clear that I do not believe God causes the awful things that happen to us, either personally or on the level of natural disasters or global pandemics. We need to be careful not to assign anything that looks like robbing, killing or destroying to God. Jesus was very clear that these things are never the work of God. God, through Jesus, is in the business of giving us life in abundance (John 10:10). That said, the beauty and power of God is that He can take the worst

[54] Margaret J Wheatley, *Leadership and the New Science: Discovering Order in a Chaotic World* (Berrett-Koehler Publishers, Oakland, 2006), p8.

things in life and create something beautiful from them. He can take death, destruction and chaos and create new life.

Resilience is not enough

In our culture, we talk a lot about resilience. Essentially, resilience is the ability to bounce back from hardship. In physics, a resilient material is one that can flex under pressure but then return to its normal state once the pressure is removed. While I'm all for building resilience so that the tough things in life don't break us, when thinking about finding meaning and purpose in the middle of winter, building resilience isn't enough. We don't want to simply flex and then 'go back to normal' when the pressure is off. What we want is to be able to change and grow. This requires not resilience, but hope. Hope helps us to find light in the darkness, to find purpose and meaning in our suffering and, dare I say it, joy too.

The hope that Jesus offers is not the wishful thinking kind that says, 'I hope things will be better next year.' There is a certainty to Christian hope because it is anchored in the promise of God that He will renew all things. This gives us hope for now and for the future. Just like light fuels the growth of a plant, the light of Jesus and the hope that He offers, that restoration and redemption are possible no matter what the circumstances of our lives, fuel our growth.

How do we grow in the middle of winter? How does God restore and redeem all that's broken and lost in our lives? In the midst of the chaos of a winter season when life feels out of control, there is one thing that we are in control of. This one thing holds the key to finding meaning and purpose in the chaos. It is the key that will unlock the door to new life and growth even in the darkest, coldest, longest winter. It is our ability to choose our response. As the psychiatrist and Nazi concentration camp survivor Viktor Frankl famously wrote, 'Everything can be taken from a man but one thing: the last of the human freedoms – to choose one's attitude in any given set of circumstances.'[55]

Surrendering the broken pieces

One of the Bible passages that I felt particularly drawn to during our winter season was Isaiah 61:1-3:

> The Spirit of the LORD God is upon me,
> because the LORD has anointed me;
> he has sent me to bring good news to the oppressed,
> to bind up the broken-hearted,
> to proclaim liberty to the captives,
> and release to the prisoners;
> to proclaim the year of the LORD'S favour ...
> to comfort all who mourn;
> to provide for those who mourn in Zion –
> to give them a garland instead of ashes,
> the oil of gladness instead of mourning,
> the mantle of praise instead of a faint spirit.

There are so many beautiful promises in this passage: the binding of the broken-hearted, release of prisoners, freedom for captives. Then there are great exchanges: a garland for ashes, the oil of gladness instead of mourning. But the key is that they are exchanges. As I reflected on the Isaiah passage during my winter season, I felt God say that, just as a beech tree surrenders its leaves to the woodland floor, I had to surrender the broken pieces of my life to Him. Rather than trying desperately to collect up all the broken pieces of my life and attempt to go back to the way things were, back to normal, I needed instead to choose to trust God with the shattered pieces of my life. To trust Him that He could birth something new from the death of my daughter. To trust that He would create a 'new normal' that

---

[55] Viktor E Frankl, *Man's Search for Meaning* (Rider, London, 2004) p75.

would be more beautiful than what I had before. To believe that with Him I could still find meaning, purpose and, crucially, hope amid the heartache.

This act of surrender may well be the hardest thing we ever have to do. As Richard Rohr says, 'surrender will always feel like dying'.[56] Yet, while surrendering ourselves to God might feel like dying, it is the path to new life.

If you doubt this, look at the Passion narratives. Surrendering to God in the Garden of Gethsemane was far from an easy thing for Jesus to do. He said to His disciples, 'My soul is overwhelmed with sorrow to the point of death' (Matthew 26:38, NIVUK). And just as we often plead for God to take us out of painful situations, Jesus prayed that God would take away the cup (Matthew 26:39). Jesus' surrender was to death – death on the cross. However, far from being the end of the story, the death of Jesus on the cross was the beginning of the greatest act of re-creation, of birthing new life, that the world has ever seen.

So, for us, perhaps, surrendering to God and taking up our cross looks like choosing to surrender the broken pieces of our lives to God in the midst of our winter season. To choose to trust in the redemptive power of God. To believe as we walk through our own Good Friday and Easter Saturday that, with God, there will always be the new life of Easter Sunday.

What is this new life that can grow from the ashes of loss? I believe it is our real life, the life God always intended for us; a life grounded on love. It is a way of living where love is the meaning of life, and our purpose is to grow in love. It is a life characterised by a desire to grow in our love of God and to live more fully into our true God-given identity as His beloved son or daughter. From this place of security, of knowing who we truly are, God calls us to love others in the way He loves us. This is what it means to live a truly human life.

---

[56] Richard Rohr, *Breathing Under Water: Spirituality and the Twelve Steps* (Franciscan Media, Cincinnati, 2011), p18.

Love is your basic all-purpose garment

It has been said by many that 'there is no such thing as bad weather, just bad clothes'. In preparation for climbing Kilimanjaro, Jon and I spent many hours in outdoor clothing shops to make sure we had the right apparel for the trek. As we ascended the mountain, it would get colder and colder, so essential to our mountain wardrobe was a good set of thermals. These thermals have since come in very handy on many a cold winter's day.

In his letter to the church at Colossae, the apostle Paul likens our new life in Christ to putting on new clothes when he tells them to 'clothe yourselves with compassion, kindness, humility, meekness, and patience' (Colossians 3:12). Paul goes on to write about the importance of love. In his paraphrase of Colossians 3, Eugene Peterson translates Paul's words this way: 'regardless of what else you put on, wear love. It's your basic, all-purpose garment' (Colossians 3:14, *The Message*). Love is our thermal base layer as we walk through winter. It is the love of God that will keep us warm as we journey through the cold and dark of the season.

Walk with me

How do we live a life grounded in love? Fortunately for us, we don't have to try to work it out on our own. God in His grace has shown us the way. The answers to these questions are found by looking at the life of Jesus. He is our model; He is the only person who has ever lived a truly and fully human life.

I love how Eugene Peterson, through *The Message* paraphrase of the Bible, has been able to breathe new life into words that may have become too familiar. This was the case for me when I first read his translation of Jesus' famous words in Matthew 11:28–30:

> Are you tired? Worn out? Burned out on religion?
> Come to me. Get away with me and you'll recover
> your life. I'll show you how to take a real rest. Walk
> with me and work with me – watch how I do it. Learn
> the unforced rhythms of grace. I won't lay anything
> heavy or ill-fitting on you. Keep company with me
> and you'll learn to live freely and lightly.

This is Jesus' invitation in every season of our lives. He invites us to come to Him, to walk with Him, to learn from Him. In return, He promises we'll recover our lives, that we'll learn to live freely and lightly. He promises that, rather than being diminished by our losses, with Him we can grow through them. What's more, in the same way that Jesus' resurrection birthed new life in others, when we start to live more fully from our true selves, we will draw others into the new life of the Kingdom too. By walking with Jesus through our winter seasons, abiding with Him, learning from Him, studying the way He did it, we can find meaning and purpose that will help us brave the elements of even the harshest of winters. Knowing that Jesus is walking with us and at work to bring new life from death will give us hope which, in turn, releases determination and perseverance to keep walking when winter seems long and the terrain is tough.

Walk it out

- In what ways are you desperately trying to cling to the broken fragments of your life? How are you attempting to 'get back to normal'?

- In the quiet, you might like to picture yourself choosing to surrender these broken pieces to Jesus.

- Spend some time with *The Message* translation of Matthew 11:28-30. Ask God to speak to you through it. What do you need to put down? What is ill-fitting?

Part 3

Walking in winter

*I will give you the treasures of darkness
and riches hidden in secret places,
so that you may know that it is I, the LORD,
the God of Israel, who call you by your name.*
Isaiah 45:3

Braving the elements

O LORD, God of my salvation,

when, at night, I cry out in your presence,

let my prayer come before you;

incline your ear to my cry.

Psalm 88:1-2

Here we are. We have 'done our research'. We have asked some hard questions of our guide – God – and of ourselves, we've thought about what the point of venturing out in winter might be, and we have clothed ourselves appropriately with a base layer of love. It sounds obvious, but the next step is actually to step out, to start walking. Tempting as it might be to simply hunker down for the winter, to hibernate and wait for it all to pass, if we want to walk on through winter, to truly experience the beauty that it has to offer, then we have to step outside. We have to brave the elements, feel the cold, face the dark, and experience the storms of the season. In terms of walking through loss, this means facing the sense of isolation and abandonment we feel and facing our anger, our hurt, our sorrow, our confusion – in short, our grief.

In his book, *A Grace Disguised*, theologian Jerry Sittser describes his journey through grief after he lost several members of his family in a car crash. It is the most beautiful and redemptive book and one of the best I have read on facing catastrophic loss.[57] At the beginning of the book, Sittser talks about how in the immediate aftermath of losing his mother, wife and daughter, he had a recurring 'waking dream'. In this dream, it was sunset, and he was desperately chasing the setting sun because he didn't want to be consumed by the darkness that would follow. When he shared this dream with his sister, she commented that the fastest way back to the light was not to chase the setting sun. Instead, it was to run headlong into the darkness of the east, knowing that you will meet the sun as it rises.[58] This beautiful image helped me hugely in my journey through loss.

It is so tempting to chase the setting sun, but this is exhausting and ultimately futile; at some point, it will get dark. There is a desperation and hopelessness about this. In contrast, there is something much more positive and hope-filled about choosing to turn to face the darkness in the knowledge that we will meet the rising sun.

Afraid of the dark

Why are we tempted to hunker down for winter? To not 'brave the elements'?

The answer is fear. As Sittser so powerfully writes, 'I was terrified by the darkness.'[59] Rather than face the dark, most of us choose to try to eliminate it. We do it with physical darkness by lighting up streets and our homes when daylight fades. We do the same with what the author, theologian, and priest Barbara Brown Taylor calls 'metaphysical darkness' – the

---

[57] Jerry Sittser, *A Grace Disguised: How the Soul Grows Through Loss*, expanded edition (Zondervan, Grand Rapids, 2004).
[58] Jerry Sittser, *A Grace Disguised*, pp41-42.
[59] Jerry Sittser, *A Grace Disguised*, p41.

psychological, emotional, relational and spiritual darkness we all experience.[60]

As I discussed previously, seasons of suffering and loss bring with them so many difficult emotions, such as anger, deep sorrow, jealousy and disappointment. On top of this, if we have a faith, we can feel spiritually confused: where is God, and why is He seemingly not doing anything to change the situation? These emotions are hard to face, and I know I worried that if I allowed myself to really feel any of them, I would be consumed by them. In many ways, the easier option did seem to avoid having to face these emotions; to hibernate, as it were, and wait for spring. The problem is that we can't bury our emotions forever. The irony is that when we refuse to face our feelings, they don't go away; rather, they grow, like mushrooms in the dark, and we end up being consumed by what we are trying to avoid.

The other problem with trying to deny or avoid emotions is that we cannot selectively turn off our feelings. Wm Paul Young writes that 'it's an all or nothing process'. When we shut down one emotion, such as sorrow, we end up shutting down all our emotions. When we do this, we 'lose the colour of life'.[61] So, tough as it is, we need to choose to feel the hard emotions so that we retain our ability to feel joy, peace and love.

I believe another reason we struggle to brave the elements of winter is that we have labelled some emotions as 'good', such as happiness, and others, like anger, as 'bad'. The reality is that emotions in and of themselves are neither good nor bad. It is what we do with our emotions, how we choose to respond to them, that matters. For example, anger is not wrong; God gets angry at injustice and oppression. What's more, the apostle Paul in his letter to the Ephesians doesn't tell the church that anger

---

[60] Barbara Brown Taylor, *Learning to Walk in the Dark*, (Canterbury Press, London, 2015), p4.
[61] Wm Paul Young, 'The Beautiful Necessity of Tears', http://wmpaulyoung.com/the-beautiful-necessity-of-tears/ (accessed 12th November 2020).

is wrong. Feeling angry is not the sin. Letting anger control us is the problem (Ephesians 4:26). We don't deal with our anger by suppressing it, because when we do this, we are still being controlled by it. Instead, our response to anger should be to recognise it, to name it, if you like, and then to choose how we respond.

It's the same with grief. Grief is not a 'bad' emotion; far from it. As the psychotherapist and writer Francis Weller so profoundly writes, 'Grief says I dared to love, that I allowed another to enter the very core of my being and find a home in my heart … it is how the soul recounts the depth to which someone has touched our lives.'[62]

Only once we have identified and named our emotions can we respond appropriately to them. If we suppress them or attempt to avoid them, they tend to come out sideways!

Choosing to express our grief rather than bury it is part of how we heal. For example, we often mistake tears as a sign of weakness, but nothing could be further from the truth. Concentration camp survivor Viktor Frankl powerfully wrote that our tears bear witness to the greatest of courage, the courage to suffer.[63] When we cry rather than attempt to bury or avoid our pain, we are facing up to it.

Interestingly, scientists have now shown that the tears we cry when we are emotional are chemically different from the tears we produce to lubricate the eyes. Emotional tears have higher levels of stress hormones and other proteins, suggesting that crying may help us relieve stress. As a result, crying may reduce our risk of health issues such as heart attacks and mental health problems. Could this be why many of us feel better after a good cry? Professor of pharmaceutics William Frey has said, 'We may feel better after crying because we are literally crying it out.

---

[62] Francis Weller, *The Wild Edge of Sorrow: Rituals of Renewal and the Sacred Work of Grief* (North Atlantic Books, 2015), p25.
[63] Viktor E Frankl, *Man's Search for Meaning*, p86.

Chemicals that build up during emotional stress may be removed in our tears when we cry.'[64]

As well as healing our physical bodies, tears are important for healing the soul. In a previous chapter, I talked about how I resonated with Mac, the main character in *The Shack*, in terms of being fed up with crying. God's response to Mac is so beautiful, encouraging Mac that tears are part of his healing. That they can articulate better than any words the movements of his heart.[65] Young unpacks this in a later blog post: 'Tears are a conduit of the spirit. They're the integration of soul and body, where what's going on inside is expressed outside.'[66] Just like the rain of winter is needed so that there is moisture in the soil for new life to grow in the spring, our tears also produce new life; the new life that comes out of healing.

Rather than burying all the emotions of grief and spiritual confusion, we need to find a healthy way to express them. How do we do this? I believe the answer lies in rediscovering the biblical practice of lament.

The Oxford Dictionary defines lament as, 'a passionate expression of grief or sorrow; a song, piece of music or poem expressing grief; a complaint'.[67] Old Testament scholar Matt Lynch defines lament as 'the brutally honest and confrontational expression of distress *before God*. It typically included acts that we'd associate with mourning – like wearing sackcloth, basic dishevelment, not eating, putting ashes on your

---

[64] William Frey quoted in Roger Dobson, 'How Crying Can Make You Healthier', *The Independent*, 11 November 2008,
https://www.independent.co.uk/life-style/health-and-families/features/how-crying-can-make-you-healthier-1009169.html (accessed 12th November 2020).

[65] Wm Paul Young, *The Shack*, p228.

[66] Wm Paul Young, 'The Beautiful Necessity of Tears'.

[67] 'Definition of lament', Oxford University Press, Lexico.com,
https://en.oxforddictionaries.com/definition/lament (accessed 12th November 2020).

head, and wailing/crying out.'[68] The fact that lament is directed to God is significant; it means that lament is worship.

The loss of lament

In his book *Hurting with God*, Glenn Pemberton makes the point that at least 40 per cent of the Psalms are laments (this is a conservative estimate; some put it as high as 70 per cent).[69] This is not even to mention Lamentations, an entire book of the Bible dedicated to lament. If you read through some of the lament Psalms, such as Psalm 6, 13, 22, 38 or 88, you will see all the dictionary definitions at work. They are passionate expressions of grief or sorrow where the writers are completely honest about how they are feeling, and – crucially – they contain complaints. Who are these words directed at? They are directed at God. For example, Psalm 13:1 says:

> How long, O LORD? Will you forget me for ever?
> How long will you hide your face from me?

Or Psalm 22:1-2, which Jesus quotes on the cross:

> My God, my God, why have you forsaken me?
> Why are you so far from helping me, from the words
> of my groaning?
> O my God, I cry by day, but you do not answer;
> and by night, but find no rest.

Moreover, the Psalms were not just there for people to read on their own; they were used in Temple worship, where they were

---

[68] Matt Lynch, 'A Time for Minor Chords: The Costly Loss of Lament in Contemporary Worship', https://wtctheology.org.uk/theomisc/time-minor-chords-costly-loss-lament-contemporary-worship/ (accessed 12th November 2020, italics added).
[69] Glenn Pemberton, *Hurting with God: Learning to Lament with the Psalms* (Abilene Christian University Press, Abilene, 2012), p32.

used as the songbook for corporate worship. In his blog post on lament, Matt Lynch 'took a cross-section of various "top hit" worship charts to look at how – and *whether* – churches in North America/UK/Australia lament'. Obviously, this was not an exhaustive survey, but the results were striking nonetheless. Of the top 100 contemporary worship songs used most commonly by churches (in a list compiled by Christian Copyright Licensing International (CCLI)) only three have any form of lament, and none of these lingers long in lament.[70]

Glenn Pemberton powerfully observes that, in our churches, 'lament is a near-dead language'.[71] This is important because, as Pemberton states, 'the songs we sing week after week influence our theology as much as, or more than, the words of a sermon or scripture itself. Our worship is not just something we do but something that transforms us.'[72]

An act of unfaith?

Why have we lost lament? Old Testament scholar Walter Brueggemann offers an answer in his book, *The Message of the Psalms*. He suggests that 'religious use of the lament psalms has been minimal because we have believed that faith does not mean to acknowledge and embrace negativity. We have thought that acknowledgement of negativity was somehow an act of unfaith, as though the very speech about it conceded too much about God's "loss of control".'[73] I resonate with this. During our winter season, when asked how I was doing, I felt like I was meant to reply along the lines of, 'I'm OK because God is present and I feel so at peace.' Don't get me wrong; on my

---

[70] Matt Lynch, 'A Time for Minor Chords: The Costly Loss of Lament in Contemporary Worship'.
[71] Glenn Pemberton, *After Lament: Psalms for Learning to Trust Again* (Abilene Christian University Press, Abilene, 2014), p33.
[72] Glenn Pemberton, *Hurting with God*, p39.
[73] Walter Brueggemann, *The Message of the Psalms: A Theological Commentary* (Augsburg Publishing House, Minneapolis, 1984), p52.

journey, there were plenty of times where I did feel God's presence and peace in the most remarkable ways, but not always. There were many days when I felt lost, anxious and alone.

But is lament an 'act of unfaith'? I am now convinced that the answer to this question is a resounding no. As Pemberton argues, 'in the Psalms, it is not those who lack faith who lament but those recognised for strong faith'.[74] If we believe in a God of love, justice and faithfulness who is sovereign, then we should be confused by the suffering and pain that both we as individuals and the world as a whole experience. Our lived experience is often at odds with what we believe to be true about God. Faith should lead us to bring all of life to God – not just the good bits.

In fact, rather than an expression of faith, trying to put a positive spin on our situation is actually making the mistake of denial, something that is ultimately not going to help us. I have just been on a rather wind-swept run, and as I was looking at the trees bending in the wind, it reminded me of the idea of resilience. For something to be resilient, it has to be able to bend; it has to be flexible. As long as it stays rigid, it is at far more risk of breaking. Denial of the reality of our situation is like being a tree in the wind that refuses to bend – it will ultimately cause us to snap.

It is hard and painful to sit in the reality of our situation, to face up to the feelings of confusion, anger and deep sadness we feel. So instead we try to rush to praise. But God wants to be in authentic relationship with us, which means He wants us to share how we're really feeling – the good, the bad and the downright ugly. As an example, just look at some of the language of Psalm 109. King David asks God to make the child of his enemy fatherless and his wife a widow (verse 9)!

Crucially, it is only once we have articulated the hurt and anger and submitted them to God that we can move on to

---

[74] Glenn Pemberton, *Hurting with God*, p33.

expressing our trust in Him and praising Him. If we lose lament, we are also in danger of losing genuine thanksgiving. We risk our thanksgiving and praise becoming hollow and more of a grin-and-bear-it exercise.

No one's listening

Refusing to be real with God about how we are feeling in the midst of pain and suffering is potentially an 'act of unfaith' in another way too. A couple of years ago, I heard the worship leader Brian Doerksen speak very powerfully about his experience of visiting a Romanian orphanage just after the Iron Curtain had come down. He describes walking into a room filled with cots, but none of the babies was crying – but not because they weren't in distress. Heartbreakingly, these children had learnt not to cry because it was of no use – no one ever came. Brian likened a Christian's inability to lament to the behaviour of these babies. He suggested that when we don't use lament as part of our worship, we are potentially behaving like these babies. We don't cry because we're not sure that there's any point to it. It's not going to cause God to respond. But the Bible tells us that we have a God who not only hears the cries of His people but that, crucially, these cries cause Him to act to rescue His people. This had a profound effect on how I viewed lament. Rather than seeing it as some kind of self-pitying whine, I began to view it as cries for help to my loving and compassionate heavenly Daddy. Like any good father, God not only hears these cries but also acts to comfort and alleviate the pain.

Keeping the lines of communication open

Finally, we have 'permission' to lament, to be real with God, because we are in a covenant relationship with Him. Because God has entered into a covenant with us in which He promises never to leave or forsake us, we have permission to remind Him of this covenant and the promises He has made when it feels like He has forgotten us. This is what many of the lament psalms do – they remind God of His covenant with Israel as a means of stimulating Him to action. To maintain our relationship with God, it is vital that we talk to Him about the things in life that call us to question His love, compassion and faithfulness – the things that leave us confused.

Think for a moment about the human covenant relationship of marriage. When a couple gets married, each party makes specific promises to the other, such as to remain faithful to each other. Because these promises have been made, it gives each party the ability to call the other to account if they suspect that these promises are not being kept. More than this, as relationship counsellors will tell you, the real problems come in a marriage when the two parties stop communicating. While they are still talking, even if this is to express anger and hurt, it means that they still care about the relationship. They haven't given up on it. It is the same with our relationship with God. Lament gives us a way of talking to God about our hurt, anger and pain; it keeps the lines of communication open.

At its heart, lament is about being in an authentic, covenant relationship with a loving God, who is faithful and just and can do something about the situation in which we find ourselves. As such, it is an act of great faith and arguably one of the most potent forms of prayer.

Calming the storm

In Luke 8:22-25, we have the account of Jesus calming a storm on the Sea of Galilee. He speaks to the wind and waves and they obey Him, leaving the disciples in awe and also afraid at just who He is that the created world should obey Him. In the Bible, water – the sea – is often used as a symbol of chaos. Right at the beginning of the Bible, God shows His power by taming the waters. He separates the waters above from the waters below. God then gathers the waters below into seas to create the dry ground (Genesis 1:6-10). When He calms the storm on the Sea of Galilee, Jesus is demonstrating that He is God, that He has the power to tame the chaos of the seas.

Lament is a way in which we can, like the disciples, call out to Jesus in the midst of our winter storms; it's a way for us to call Him to action in our lives. If we can cry out in honesty to Jesus, just like the disciples did, we'll see Him calm our storms. We'll witness Him replace anxiety with peace, despair with hope, and turn our darkness to light and so help us to reorient ourselves.

Just like each winter brings with it more than one storm, the storms of our emotions will keep coming. What's more, just like on the Sea of Galilee, where storms can seemingly come from nowhere, we're likely to be hit by a storm when we least expect it. In my experience, it's not the things that I think will bring grief back up to the surface that actually do. I guess that's because, in a way, I'm psychologically prepared for them. It's the things that come out of nowhere that release the storms in me. We don't lament just once; it's a practice we have to keep coming back to. If we are to walk on through winter, we have to keep stepping out into the elements and expressing to God all we are feeling. His promise to us is that He is with us, He hears us, and He will respond.

Walk it out

- Rather than braving the elements of your emotions, how have you attempted to hibernate through winter? What prevents you from expressing your feelings?

- What is your initial reaction to the concept of complaining to God? If you haven't ever practised lament, what stops you?

- If you are in the midst of a winter season as you read this, spend some time with the words of Psalm 13. Make them your prayer as you brave the elements of winter.

Casting our cares

Cast all your anxiety on him, because he cares for you.

1 Peter 5:7

How do we actually practise lament? If we look through the laments in the Psalms we can see that, with rare exceptions, there is a consistent pattern to their structure that can be divided into two parts: 1) plea, and 2) praise.[75] I want to focus in on the first part of this: plea. To illustrate this, I am going to use one of the lament psalms: Psalm 69. This Psalm is illustrative of other biblical laments in that the plea contains a complaint, an appeal for intervention, motivation for doing so and an imprecation where the writer is very candid about how they want God to act to resolve the situation. As I have said before, crucially, all of the above are addressed to God. Using the acronym CAST, as in, 'Cast all your anxiety on him, because he cares for you,'[76] let's work through each one in turn.

---

[75] Claus Westermann, quoted in Brueggemann, *The Message of the Psalms*, p54.
[76] I have adapted teaching by Rick Warren on lament in which he uses a similar acronym – CARE, based on 1 Peter 5:7.

C = Complain

Describe the problem to God as honestly as you can. Just after Libby died, I spent time with these verses from Psalm 69:

> Save me, O God,
> for the waters have come up to my neck.
> I sink in deep mire,
> where there is no foothold;
> I have come into deep waters,
> and the flood sweeps over me.
> I am weary with my crying;
> my throat is parched.
> My eyes grow dim
> with waiting for my God.
> *Psalm 69:1-3*

Grief is really tiring and, as I have said previously, I got to a point where I was thoroughly fed up with crying. While I didn't have physical enemies in the form of people attacking me, I did feel the reality of the spiritual battle. It was a battle for hope, and this was exhausting. I did feel like I was sinking in the mud, being overwhelmed by the floodwaters of grief.

In biblical laments, part of the point of the complaint is to turn the author's problem into a problem for God, because He is the one 'who is both able and responsible for doing something about it'.[77] We see this in Psalm 69, where it is clear that David blames the absence of God's help for the continuation of problems he is facing.

I have always found writing to be a constructive means of processing my emotions. So one of the ways that I was able to complain to God in this midst of all that we went through was to write Him a letter. In this letter, I laid bare all of my feelings of grief, anger, abandonment and betrayal. I questioned God as to why He was allowing me to go through all of this; why wasn't

---

[77] Walter Brueggemann, *The Message of the Psalms*, p54.

He doing something to alleviate the intense pressure I felt under?

A = Appeal

This is a plea for God to intervene on our behalf because the situation we are facing is too big for us to handle. We see this repeatedly in Psalm 69, where David appeals to God to rescue him from sinking in the mud, from drowning in deep waters or from the pit of death. I certainly felt that I was at risk of being overwhelmed by my pain; I felt helpless in the face of it. I definitely appealed to God to get me out, to help me, because I was sinking under the weight of my grief.

S = Stimulate

In their petitions for God's intervention, the psalmists also provide reasons why God should intervene, which they hope will stimulate Him to act on their behalf. These motivations range from reminders of God's covenant promises to very personal cries that the author of the lament is close to death as a result of all that they are facing. Therefore, there is an urgent need for God to intervene (as in Psalm 69:15). While this might seem melodramatic at times, I really did feel as though I was in a battle for my life. There were points along the way where I contemplated death, as it felt like it would have been easier.

Another way in which the authors of biblical laments attempt to stimulate God to action is to suggest that God needs to consider His own reputation.[78] Although it might seem less than noble, when Jon and I were walking through our season of loss, one of our regular prayers was that God would rescue us from our situation because His reputation was on the line. He needed to prove to us, and to all those around us, that He was

---

[78] Walter Brueggemann, *The Message of the Psalms*, p55.

who He said He was. This echoes another lament Psalm where David prays, 'For your name's sake, O LORD, preserve my life' (Psalm 143:11).

Writers of the laments also regularly appeal to God's character as a means of stimulating Him into action. For example, in Psalm 69 we repeatedly see David appealing to God's great love and mercy as a reason for Him to act (verses 13, 16).

T = Tell

The Psalms permit us to be really honest; the writers do not hold back in telling God how they want Him to act to avenge the wrong that has been done. In Psalm 69, as well as asking God to rescue him, David prays that his enemies' eyes would 'be darkened so that they cannot see, and ... their loins tremble continually' (verse 23). He goes on to ask God to pour out his wrath on them (verse 24). Language like this can sound shocking to our modern sensibilities. In fact, this has been one of the reasons that Christians have shied away from praying what are known as the Psalms of Imprecation.[79] However, there is a brutal honesty to this language.

Who among us would not admit to wanting to exact revenge when we have been wronged in some way, or when we witness those close to us suffering brutality? From a Christian perspective, I would argue that it is far better for us to pour out these emotions and desires to God than to let them fester and potentially grow into either hatred of a person or group of people, or into bitterness and resentment about a situation in which we find ourselves.

I did spend a lot of time in the early days after Libby died telling God how He could get me out of the pain that I was in.

[79] Gordon Wenham, Chapter 6, 'The Imprecatory Psalms', in *The Psalter Reclaimed: Praying and Praising with the Psalms* (Crossway Books, 2013, accessed from Scribd (www.scribd.com)).

Mainly this involved pleading with Him to make sure it would not be long until we had another child. I also have to admit to feelings of anger towards the medical staff who looked after me during my pregnancy. Jon and I have often reflected on the fact that while Libby's death was a tough thing for my consultant to have to face, it is unlikely to have impacted his life to the extent that our lives have been affected. Libby's death has left a hole that we will live with for the rest of our lives. I thought of exacting revenge on those I blamed for Libby's death in the form of legal proceedings against them. I wanted to make them share some of the pain that I feel. It is vital to acknowledge these feelings, and I believe that the safest place to take them is to God.

In summary, it is only having gone through these four stages of complain, appeal, stimulate and tell, that Psalms of lament make the turn from plea to praise. With rare exceptions, biblical laments do make this shift, but only once they have faced up to the reality of the situation.

By using this pattern, lament is not about self-pity or wallowing; instead, it's about being real before God about the situation we're in, asking God to intervene because we know He can, and expressing trust in Him in the midst of the crisis. When I was in the pain and brokenness of all our losses, I found that lament gave me a means of authentically communicating with God.

Weeping with those who weep

As the apostle Paul encourages us, authentic Christian community is about weeping with those who weep as well as rejoicing with those who rejoice (Romans 12:15). We need to be able to hold lament and praise together. As Chris Green articulates, faith means we believe that God is equally involved in all things everywhere, always.[80] It doesn't matter whether those things are, as we see them, good or full of pain and suffering, God is right there in every situation. Therefore, there will always be something to praise Him for and always something to lament.

To call those who are weeping to rejoice with those who are praising is a big ask. It is the equivalent of asking me to praise God for the safe arrival of a baby in the wake of the death of my child. But this is what we are called to do.

However, I believe it is equally challenging to enter authentically and fully into the pain of others – to do what Jesus did at Lazarus' tomb, to be so full of compassion for others that we weep with them. Weeping with others is costly, but it is a crucial part of our witness as believers. As the New Testament theologian Tom Wright powerfully articulates in the book *God and the Pandemic*, when awful things happen in the world, rather than trying to work out why it's happening or telling people that God is using these things as a means of calling them to repentance, the Church should stand in the solidarity of lament with the world.[81]

I believe lament gives us a powerful means of standing in solidarity with all those who are suffering in our fractured world. It provides us with the ability to cry out to God about all the brokenness we see around us and to appeal to Him to intervene. This is not just about when things such as global pandemics break out. We are called to cry out for those who are oppressed, victims of injustice, the poor and the marginalised. The Psalms of Imprecation, such as Psalm 109, are 'an eloquent affirmation of God's compassion for the poor and needy ... God's fundamental character is to stand with and for the poor and

---

[80] Chris Green, 'God's Sovereignty and Our Freedom', Every Day Theology podcast episode 21, 21 May 2020.
[81] Tom Wright, *God and the Pandemic: A Christian Reflection on the Coronavirus and its Aftermath* (SPCK, London, 2020), p13.

needy. To be instructed by Psalm 109 is to take our stand with God and the poor and needy.'[82]

For all these reasons, lament needs to be part of our corporate worship. Obviously, this includes sung worship, but there are other ways to incorporate lament – for example, in our prayers of intercession. I regularly speak on the importance of lament, and I am always moved by people's reaction to essentially being given permission to be real with God. After one such talk, a wonderful man called Richard sent me an email. He had been inspired to incorporate a prayer of lament into his intercessions on Mothering Sunday. As I know only too well, alongside being a day to be thankful for our mothers, Mothering Sunday can be a really tough day for many people in a variety of different ways. In his email, Richard said that he had been overwhelmed by the response he had received after the service. In his words, 'there were simply heaps of people that came and thanked me afterwards – male and female, old and young'.

Richard has very kindly permitted me to include his lament here, and I can think of no better way to end this chapter than with his words:

> Eternal God, Lord and giver of life,
> We give thanks that You
> Are totally and utterly dependable.
>
> Yet
> While we celebrate and give thanks for Mums
> And all that they do and all that they are,
>
> We Also Remember Those:
>
> Who are Mothers but have lost their children,
> Where there is no one to call out 'Mum'
> And

---

[82] Clinton McCann, quoted in Gordon Wenham, *The Psalter Reclaimed*, p170.

Those whose won't see their Mum today
Through bereavement or separation or circumstance.

We Remember:
Those who never knew their Mum at all
And
Those who are not able to be a Mum

These things make our hearts hurt and our eyes to sting
And cause us to ask questions no one can answer

But we know You are the one who
Hides us under the Shadow of Your Wing …
Who is closer than our breath …
Who holds us in the palm of Your hand …
And who sings over us,
Just like a Mum would do.

So we thank You
For Your love that never fails …
For Your presence from which we can never be separated …
And Your peace which transcends our understanding …

We are grateful for
The huge family of God that You put us in
Where we can cry with those in pain
And
Share joy with those who celebrate
Thanking You today for the precious gift to us
of Motherhood and Mums.
Amen.

- If you find writing a helpful way to process emotions, you might want to try writing a really honest letter to God expressing how you are feeling, including any desire for revenge or any unexpressed bitterness, and appealing to God to act. Alternatively, you might be inspired to write your own poem of lament.

- Others, who don't find writing helpful as a way of processing emotion, may find it beneficial to talk it out with God. I have one friend who used to go to deserted beaches to, in her words, 'rant at God'. You could try this!

- Is there a particular group of people or a global situation that God has placed on your heart? Could you use lament as a way of standing in solidarity with these people and asking God to act on their behalf?

Embrace winter

When I was at school, I had the most wonderful form tutor called Mrs Wharton. On our last day in her class, she gave us all a little gift. For most of the students, this was some kind of chocolate. As the caring lady she was, Mrs Wharton knew that I didn't eat chocolate (I'm sure you're asking yourself, 'Who doesn't eat chocolate?!'). So instead she gave me a bookmark with the words of the Serenity Prayer written on it. Many of you will be familiar with these words:

> God grant me the serenity
> To accept the things I cannot change;
> Courage to change the things I can;
> And wisdom to know the difference.
> Living one day at a time;
> Enjoying one moment at a time;
> Accepting hardships as the pathway to peace;
> Taking, as He did, this sinful world
> As it is,
> Not as I would have it;
> Trusting that He will make all things right
> If I surrender to His Will;

So that I may be reasonably happy in this life
And supremely happy with Him
Forever and ever in the next
Amen.[83]

As I ponder these words again, I am struck by how prophetic my teacher's gift to me all those years ago was. These were the words that I needed to be able to put into practice in my life as I walked through winter.

Accepting hardships

If you are familiar with Elizabeth Kübler-Ross' five stages of grief, you will know that one of the stages is acceptance. Kübler-Ross talks about how those who can reach some level of acceptance when it comes to loss or dying find that it brings peace. For myself, acceptance of the losses I have faced has been vital in my journey through grief and has helped me find peace.

I have talked in a previous chapter about how one of the questions I asked when Libby died, and when we lost other babies through miscarriage, was, 'Why us?' After Libby died, I had the privilege of spending time with an amazing Christian lady who sadly had experienced a similar loss to mine. Just six months before Libby died, she and her husband's first son was stillborn at full term. Something she said really hit home for me. Rather than asking, 'Why me?' she said the question should be, 'Why not me?'

Just sit with those words for a moment and the power of them. This is acceptance in its most real and heartbreaking form. This kind of acceptance is about 'taking … this sinful world as it is'.

So often I think we make the mistake of thinking that, as Christians, we should be immune to life's tragedies and pain.

---

[83] Reinhold Niebuhr, *The Serenity Prayer* (1943).

However, this is not what Jesus taught. He actually said the opposite: 'Here on earth you will have many trials and sorrows' (John 16:33, NLT). So, hard as it sounds, no one gets a free pass from the pain, brokenness and loss of this world.

Acceptance is not enough

Harsh as it might sound, I don't believe that acceptance of our situations is enough. I came to this conclusion after reading *The Message* translation of Luke 9:23-25. In this famous passage, Jesus talks about the cost of following Him and how we must all take up our cross. I remember being stunned by the words of Jesus in this paraphrase: 'Don't run from suffering; embrace it. Follow me and I'll show you how.' Personally, I might just be able to begin to accept suffering, but embracing it seems like a step too far. It feels like some form of self-punishment. Who embraces suffering?

Jesus did.

Jesus didn't run from suffering. Instead, He embraced the cross; the most brutal form of suffering and death that the Romans could come up with, and they were pretty good when it came to torturing and killing people. On the cross, Jesus both faced down and embraced the darkness of this world. He embraced all of the brokenness and sin of the world as He died on the cross.

The necessary fall

The question remains, why would Jesus embrace suffering? I think the answer circles back to how new life is released. As Richard Rohr powerfully articulates in his book *Falling Upward*, 'the way up is the way down'.[84] The route to new life is through

---

[84] Richard Rohr, *Falling Upward: A Spirituality for the Two Halves of Life* (SPCK, London, 2012), p xvii.

a necessary falling; it is through death. Jesus was able to embrace the brutality and suffering of the cross because He knew that it was in the going down, into death, that new life would be birthed. Going down to go up is what St Augustine called the 'paschal mystery'. It is the mystery of Easter and, as Rohr says, it makes no sense to our western philosophy of progress and upward mobility.[85]

It is this paradoxical truth that suffering and death are necessary for the release of the new life of the Kingdom in us that led the apostle James to write, 'whenever you face trials of any kind, consider it nothing but joy' (James 1:2). In the King James translation of these verses, James goes on to write that trials in life make us perfect. The word translated 'perfect' is the Greek word *teleios*, which means brought to its end, wanting nothing, completeness. What is our 'end'? It is to become like Jesus. In God's hands, pain and suffering perfect us because they help us to grow in Christlikeness.

That said, at the risk of sounding like a broken record, God does not cause the pain and loss in our lives. He doesn't need to do that in order to release new life.

A tough nut

So why is the fall necessary? Why do we have to go down in order to go up? The answer lies in the truth that only great pain or great love are strong enough to strip away the layers of our false selves to reveal our true selves. The fall is necessary because the false self is a tough nut to crack, in part because it is not all bad. It often serves us well, helping us to feel safe, secure and in control. The problem is that the false self is built on the prop of ego, where we base our identity on what we have, what others say about us or what we do. The false self is all about self-sufficiency and separateness, whereas the true self is

---

[85] Richard Rohr, *Falling Upward*, p xxi.

defined by communion and contentment.[86] Communion with God allows us to rediscover our belovedness and to root our lives in His love for us. When we do this, we find real contentment, and we grow in an ever-deeper measure into our true God-given identities.

Constantly fighting against our winter season will leave us locked in the false self. We will desperately try to remain self-sufficient, to force our way out of winter, to find our own solutions, to re-establish control (which, by the way, we never had anyway!) and get life back to normal. Living this way keeps us disconnected from God and from experiencing His love and is, quite frankly, exhausting!

We can't ever engineer our own falls. Actually, we don't have to because, as I have said, in this broken world, the fall will come – for most of us in the form of the pain of loss. Our role when the fall comes is not to respond from the ego and look to control the situation, but instead to embrace our winter season by trusting in God and His love – knowing that the fall is necessary in order to release new life in us. That said, dying to the false self and living life from the true self, which is rooted in God's love, is not a once-in-a-lifetime thing. Rather than one death, it is a series of mini deaths.

Climbing the mountain

When we climbed Kilimanjaro, the walking itself was not that difficult. Much to my relief, no rock climbing was required! The hard part was getting used to the altitude. A failure to acclimatise to the reduced oxygen levels is the reason that many people do not make it to the summit.

One of the main ways a climber can avoid this issue is by taking time to ascend, giving their body time to adjust. It was for this reason that, rather than walking a route that would take only three days to reach the summit, we chose a route that took

---

[86] Richard Rohr, *True Self False Self* (audio recording, 2010).

five days. The strategy was to climb high, sleep low, thus helping our bodies acclimatise to the altitude. On several of the days, we would climb until lunchtime and then descend slightly in the afternoon.

In addition to our choice of route, our guides made us walk much more slowly than we would otherwise have chosen to. Their favourite phrase was *pole pole*, which means 'slowly, slowly' in Swahili. Those who rush to reach the summit are more often the ones who fail to make it because they don't give their bodies time to adjust to the altitude.

I find this a helpful metaphor when thinking about our journey from living in the false self to living in greater union with Jesus, and hence living from our true selves. We make a little progress, we climb for a bit, but then we fall back again. The falling can feel depressing at the time, it can feel like we are not making progress, but we are. Each time we climb, we get a little higher.

Much like adjusting to the altitude, it takes time to adjust to a life rooted in God's love. We can't rush the process, mainly because it is so countercultural. Just as we had our guides on the mountain, we have a guide in the form of the Holy Spirit. He knows the terrain, and He knows us better than we know ourselves. Our job is to allow the Spirit to lead, and to walk in step with Him, to go at His pace, not ours (see Galatians 5:25).

Just as walking slowly meant that we were on Kilimanjaro longer, going at God's pace in terms of letting go of the false self will often mean that we have to stay in winter longer than we would want to. In the next chapter, I want to explore further why it's important not to rush this process. For now, I simply want to say that if we can embrace winter by understanding that it is necessary for the release of new life, we will be able to trust God with the timing of this process.

Walk it out

- What is your initial response to the idea of embracing suffering?

- What is your reaction to the idea that a fall is necessary for our spiritual growth?

- Spend some time reflecting on Jesus' words in *The Message* translation of Luke 9:23-25:

> Anyone who intends to come with me has to let me lead. You're not in the driver's seat – I am. Don't run from suffering; embrace it. Follow me and I'll show you how. Self-help is no help at all. Self-sacrifice is the way, *my* way, to finding yourself, your true self. What good would it do to get everything you want and lose you, the real you?

There are no shortcuts

The fruit of the Spirit is love, joy, peace, patience, kindness, generosity, faithfulness, gentleness, and self-control.

Galatians 5:22-23

Much like the beginning of winter, when the coronavirus lockdown started in the UK, I was in the fortunate position of being able to enjoy the novelty of it. Like so many people, I was exhausted with the crazy pace of life and I enjoyed the opportunity to slow down, to spend time at home with Jon and Charlie. There was no FOMO because there was literally nothing to miss out on! Yet while there were many things about the enforced slowdown that I liked and wanted to keep when we emerged on the other side of it, such as the fact that life was generally simpler and less hurried, I regularly had days when I longed for us to be through the crisis. I missed being able to see my family or popping down to our local pub. I struggled with the uncertainty of not knowing when or if school would restart for Charlie, or what the impact of the pandemic would be on my work.

Once the novelty of it all wore off, the reality began set in for many people. As a result of lockdown, the UK economy shrunk by 20 per cent in April 2020.[87] Many people found themselves out of work or struggling to keep their businesses afloat. For example, a friend of mine told me about someone they knew who had seen the business that they had worked so hard to grow disappear pretty much overnight as a result of the national shutdown. Not surprisingly, this person went on to struggle with their mental health.

There were parents who struggled to juggle homeschooling with their paid work for months on end. Then there are thousands of people around the country (and the world) whose loved ones died and who had to grieve alone. As the reality of the scale of the losses set in, winter really began to bite.

In this context, I think it's totally normal to look for the fastest way out of winter, to find a shortcut out of the pain. In a sense, we are desperately searching for signs of spring. A number of years ago I worked in vaccine development and I, like the rest of the world, spent a lot of the summer of 2020 desperately hoping that my former colleagues would be able to develop a vaccine that would put an end to the pandemic.

Being grounded

During the coronavirus crisis, I heard a podcast with Mo Gawdat, the former Chief Business Officer at Google X (the innovation arm of Google) and author of the book *Solve for Happy: Engineer Your Path to Joy*.[88] In this podcast, Mo relayed a conversation he had with his adult daughter at the beginning of lockdown in the US. Her take on the crisis was that whether you chose to call it God or the universe, it was like we had all been

---

[87] 'Bank of England "ready to act" as economy shrinks record 20%', BBC News, https://www.bbc.co.uk/news/business-53019360 (accessed 3rd December 2020).

[88] Mo Gawdat, *Solve for Happy: Engineer Your Path to Joy* (Bluebird, London, 2019).

grounded. We had been sent to our rooms to think about what we'd been doing.[89]

In one sense, I would agree with this sentiment. Global lockdown did give us all a chance to re-evaluate life. And in the midst of it, it gave the planet room to breathe, with polluted skies clearing and carbon dioxide emissions falling (if only temporarily).

However, we paid a very high price for these benefits. As I have repeated throughout this book, I don't believe that God ever causes awful things like a pandemic, or the death of a loved one, or the loss of a livelihood. He does not cause or lead us into winter seasons of suffering. These awful things are not God punishing us, nor are they part of a divine spiritual formation plan where the dreadful things that happen are necessary for our spiritual growth.

All of that said, I do believe that God does on occasions allow us to experience the consequences of our actions. In the Old Testament, we see this when the people of Israel are exiled from their land. Their exile was not punishment by God but more the simple consequence of them continually deciding to go their own way.

One of the verses that people often gave me in the wake of Libby's death was from Jeremiah 29, where God speaks through the prophet Jeremiah to the exiled people of Judah. It is familiar to many:

> For surely I know the plans I have for you, says the
> LORD, plans for your welfare and not for harm, to
> give you a future with hope.
> *Jeremiah 29:11*

These are beautiful, hope-filled words that anyone living in the midst of winter needs to hear. We all need to know that God

---

[89] Mo Gawdat, quoted in 'How to Fail with Elizabeth Day' podcast, released 23rd March 2020, https://howtofail.podbean.com/e/how-to-fail-mo-gawdat/ (accessed 12th November 2020).

has not forgotten us, that He has good plans for our lives. However, I have often wondered about the context of this verse. So when it popped up on social media feeds at the beginning of the coronavirus pandemic, I decided to have a look.

What I discovered was really challenging. In the previous chapter of the book of Jeremiah, the false prophet Hananiah has been misleading the people of Judah. He has told them that God will liberate them from exile in Babylon within two years (Jeremiah 28:1-4). Basically, Hananiah was giving the nation false hope of a quick exit from exile. Into this context, Jeremiah writes to the exiles, telling them that some prophets and fortune-tellers are telling lies. Their exile will not last just two years, but seventy years (Jeremiah 29:10). Through Jeremiah, God instructs the people to:

> Build houses and live in them; plant gardens and eat what they produce. Take wives and have sons and daughters; take wives for your sons, and give your daughters in marriage, that they may bear sons and daughters; multiply there, and do not decrease.
> *Jeremiah 29:5-6*

God is telling the people of Israel not to look for the exit or a shortcut. Instead, He calls them to settle into exile. This a profoundly challenging message when we find ourselves in the midst of a winter season that is painful and feels like it will never end. During our winter season of baby loss, the last thing I wanted to do was settle down into the exile it had caused. I wanted to find the fastest way out of winter into spring.

Why does God ask us to settle into our winter season of exile? What is wrong with looking for a quick way out?

Gifts are given; fruit grows

As we have seen, winter seasons of death and loss can birth new life in us, a new life rooted in and lived out of the love of God. Essentially, this growth into a life of love is the process of spiritual formation. In his profound book, *Invitation to a Journey*, New Testament Professor Robert Mulholland defines spiritual formation as 'the process of being formed in the image of Christ for the sake of others'.[90] Within certain streams of the Church, we have often been guilty of confusing salvation with sanctification. Salvation is the free gift of God through the life, death and resurrection of Jesus. We are reconciled, made right with God, by faith in Jesus alone (see Romans 1:17; Ephesians 2:8-9). We do nothing to deserve or earn this; it is a gift from God.

Sanctification, on the other hand, is a process: the process of growing in Christlikeness and therefore into a truly human life. It is the process of spiritual formation. In essence, it is the growth of the fruit of the Spirit in our lives. Unlike salvation, which is a gift we receive when we confess our belief in Jesus, sanctification is the journey of a lifetime.

As I said, I grew up in the charismatic stream of the Church. In this setting, a lot of emphasis was put on the gifts of the Spirit, such as the prophetic, speaking in tongues and healing. All of these things are beautiful gifts that we should ask for and receive with gratitude and joy from our heavenly Father. What wasn't talked about so much was the fruit of the Spirit: 'love, joy, peace, patience, kindness, generosity, faithfulness, gentleness, and self-control' (Galatians 5:22-23).

As I have reflected on this, I find myself wondering whether this isn't in part a result of the instant society in which we live, where we can order something online late at night and have it

---

[90] M Robert Mulholland Jr, *Invitation to a Journey: A Road Map for Spiritual Formation*, expanded edition (InterVarsity Press, Downers Grove, 2016), p16.

delivered the next day. Or we can sit down in front of Netflix and find a film to watch rather than having to go out to the video rental shop (some of you reading are wondering what on earth a video rental shop is – count yourself lucky that you are that young!).

Perhaps we like the gifts of the Spirit because they are given; we simply have to ask for them. The fruit of the Spirit is harder because, rather than being given, fruit grows; there is a process involved. While this process is initiated and empowered by the Spirit, it takes some effort on our part. This process of sanctification is still a work of grace in our lives but one in which we participate. As the philosopher and writer, Dallas Willard said, 'grace is opposed to earning, not to effort.'[91]

The valley

Added to the realisation that fruit grows is the truth that most crops are grown on plains or in valleys, not on mountaintops. What is physically true of crops is also spiritually true in our lives. It is not during mountaintop experiences that we get to grow the fruit of the Spirit; it's in the valleys of life. Nicholas Wolterstorff is a philosopher and teacher at Yale whose adult son died in a mountain-climbing accident. He powerfully articulates the truth that the fruit of the Spirit grows in the valley: 'in the valley of suffering … character is made. The valley of suffering is the vale of soul-making.'[92] Or, as the apostle Paul writes in his letter to the church in Rome, 'suffering produces endurance, and endurance produces character, and character produces hope' (Romans 5:3-4).

---

[91] Dallas Willard, *The Great Omission: Reclaiming Jesus' Essential Teachings on Discipleship* (Monarch Books, Oxford, 2006) p34.
[92] Nicholas Wolterstorff, quoted in Jerry Sittser, *A Grace Disguised*, p49.

It takes time

Like many people, the slower pace of life created by the coronavirus lockdown meant that I finally got around to doing some things I had been meaning to do for a while, one of which was growing my own vegetables. I guess I did listen to God's call to the people in exile to 'plant gardens and eat what they produce' (Jeremiah 29:5). In early spring, Charlie and I planted tiny lettuce, radish, beetroot, courgette, French bean and tomato seeds. We lovingly tended these in our glazed porch area inside the house, then transplanted them into larger pots and finally planted them in our raised bed when the threat of frost was over. By June we were, at last, getting some home-grown produce. Growing our own fruit and vegetables was a very satisfying thing to do, but it also showed me again how slow the growth process in nature is. It took weeks and, in some cases, months, before we saw any fruit from our labours.

What's more, the growth process couldn't be rushed. I couldn't will a plant to grow any faster, no matter how much plant food and water I gave it. And if I had rushed to plant tomatoes out too early, chances are they would have been 'got' by frost, the result being that they would not have produced anything like the harvest we did have.

Spiritual formation is the same; it takes time – a lot of time! And we can't rush it. What's more, we can't bring about our growth in Christlikeness through our own willpower. It is not our willpower that will grow this in us; it is the power of the Spirit at work in our lives. Our role is simply to be open and willing to allow the Spirit to do His work.

If we try to rush the process, to force our way into spring before winter is over, we risk losing some of the fruit that God can grow in these times. Not long after Libby died, a wonderfully wise friend, someone who was no stranger to heartbreak having lost their wife to cancer, very movingly said to me, 'Sometimes we have to stay in a place of pain longer than we would want to in order to receive the healing that God has for us.'

Much as we might like to rush on, we are called to 'be guided by the Spirit' (Galatians 5:25). Just like the people of Judah were not in exile for forever, our winter season will pass, and spring will come. During winter, our job is to trust God with the timing of the season change.

Living with unintended consequences

As well as potentially losing some of the fruit that God wants to grow in our lives through the process of spiritual formation, trying to find a shortcut out of winter with our own solution can result in other problems.

One of the biblical stories that helped me during our winter season was the story of Abraham and Sarah (see Genesis 12; 15–18; 21). I felt a real affiliation to Sarah as we journeyed through our winter season. She is a woman who can't have children. Then, in her old age, her husband Abraham receives a promise from God that their descendants will be more numerous than the stars in the sky. The kicker is that from the point at which God promises this, Abraham and Sarah have to wait more than twenty-five years. Having had to wait six years for the fulfilment of our promise, I can't even begin to imagine what it would be like to wait twenty-five years. What's more, this time frame doesn't even take into account all the long years before God made the promise. Scholars estimate that Sarah was already over sixty when God spoke to Abraham.

Sarah is an example of what happens when we try to rush the promises of God, when we try to find a shortcut out of our pain. In the biblical account, after waiting several years for God to fulfil His promise, Sarah takes matters into her own hands. She gives her servant Hagar to Abraham, the result being that Hagar conceives a son, Ishmael (Genesis 16). It would be easy to judge Sarah, but I understand something of her desperation. We are told that she is already seventy-five years old and it has been several years since God promised her a son. Add to this the cultural shame that she would feel as a woman unable to conceive, and we should feel more compassionate towards her.

One of the things I love about this story is how gracious and faithful God is to Sarah, despite her lack of faith. God doesn't take back His promise; in fact, He reiterates His promise to Abraham that he and Sarah will have a child. He finally fulfils this promise some fourteen years later when Isaac is born, by which point Abraham is 100 years old and Sarah is over ninety.

While I might understand and empathise with Sarah trying to fix the problem herself, as the theologian Paula Gooder says, 'the problem, of course, with desperate actions is living with their consequences'.[93] For Sarah, the consequence is family discord and jealousy, leading her to force Abraham to send Hagar and Ishmael away with the words, 'Cast out this slave woman with her son; for the son of this slave woman shall not inherit along with my son Isaac' (Genesis 21:10). I have often thought about Hagar and how the consequences of Sarah (and Abraham's) poor decision-making are far worse for her than for Sarah. She is used to produce a son and twice thrown out of the household into the desert. If it weren't for the grace of God, both she and her son would have died.

Similar to the promise God made to Abraham, I really believed that God had given us a promise that we would have another child after Libby. When I was tempted to try to find a shortcut to the fulfilment of this promise, in order to fulfil my desperate desire to have a child, Sarah's story served as a check to my desire. If I had chosen to seek a human solution to my problem, it wouldn't necessarily have annulled the promise of God, but it might have had unforeseen and unwanted consequences, ones that potentially could have affected not just me but others, things I would have had to live with for the rest of my life. It has been said that wisdom is making a decision

---

[93] Paula Gooder, *The Meaning is in the Waiting: The Spirit of Advent* (Canterbury Press, London, 2008), p27.

that we will be happy with in the future. It requires lifting our eyes from the current situation to look at the long game. Thinking this way helped me to slow down and consider the consequences of my actions.

Missing what's right in front of you

Confession time: I live a lot of my life in my head. I'm either ruminating on things that have happened in the past or thinking and planning for the future. I find it very difficult to live in the present moment. For example, I can be playing with Charlie and, while I am physically present, mentally I am somewhere else entirely. It might be something as mundane as thinking about grocery shopping or what we're going to eat for supper, or I might be flicking through my phone. Or it could be a more significant concern about a project at work, or a relationship worry I have. Either way, I am not fully present with Charlie.

In these times I'm more likely to miss important things he says to me, either because I'm not genuinely listening or because I haven't asked him in the first place. I'm also going to miss the little moments of joy that come from shared experiences. In essence, I'm going to miss out on the depth of relationship that is possible when I give my whole attention to him.

It is the same with our relationship with God. If we give too much attention to focusing on the fulfilment of a promise – basically looking for the end of winter – we miss being present to God in the midst of our situation. We miss the depth of relationship with Him that He longs for us to experience. We miss the opportunity to know and be known. We lose the chance for real connection. Like my interactions with Charlie, if we are focused on getting out of winter, we will find it hard to hear the 'gentle whisper' (1 Kings 19:12, NIVUK) of our loving Father above all the internal chatter.

Deciding to stay in winter is hard. There were many days where I didn't manage it. Days spent on the computer googling all the different ways around the problem we had. But these were not the days when I felt at peace. In fact, they were among my most anxious and unhappy times. The days when I resolved to live more fully present to God, when I allowed myself to experience His love and presence in the midst of winter, were the days that I felt most at peace. It was on these days that I could 'trust the process', as my mum often likes to say. I was able to trust God that He was in the process of growing new life from the ashes of my old life, that I could trust in His faithfulness, that He would fulfil His promise to me, in His way and in His time. I could also trust Him that there would be fruit from this season – hard though the season was.

Walk it out

- What are the ways that you are tempted to rush out of winter, to find a shortcut? How might these have unintended consequences for you and those around you?

- You might like to reflect on the list of the fruit of the Spirit (Galatians 5:22-23). Which of these would you like to grow in your life?

- Rather than constantly living in the past or the future, trying to escape where we are, but instead staying present to God in each day, you might find it helpful to pray with the Examen. This is form of prayer used at the end of each day to help us recognise how God has been present throughout our day.[94]

---

[94] For a great introduction to the Prayer of Examen please see, 'How can I pray?' https://www.ignatianspirituality.com/ignatian-prayer/the-examen/how-can-i-pray/ (accessed 13th February 2021).

Stick with your guide

I am the way, the truth, and the life.

John 14:6

Eighteen months after Libby died, Jon and I found ourselves sitting and waiting for yet another consultant appointment, this time to discuss the process for IVF treatment. To fill time while waiting, I was reading American pastor and theologian Timothy Keller's book on the Gospel of Mark.[95] I found myself reading the account of Jesus' interaction with a paralysed man who had some amazingly persistent friends. Rather than being deterred by a room full to bursting, they made a hole in the roof and lowered him to Jesus (Mark 2:1-12). I've often wondered what the owner of the house might have felt about this.

Intriguingly, and very controversially for those in the room, the first words that Jesus said to the paralysed man were not about his physical healing. His first words were 'Son, your sins are forgiven' (Mark 2:5). An argument ensued with the scribes who were present. The scribes were outraged because only God can forgive sins, so in telling the man that his sins were forgiven, Jesus was claiming to be God.

In his unpacking of this healing, Keller articulates the truth that while the paralysed man probably thought that his biggest

---

[95] Timothy Keller, *King's Cross: Understanding the Life and Death of the Son of God* (Hodder & Stoughton, London, 2011).

problem was his paralysis, Jesus knew that this was not the case. The real problem was with the state of the man's heart. What he needed most was to know that his sins were forgiven.[96] He needed to know that he was reconciled to God, that there was nothing separating him from God's love. You probably know the end of the story – Jesus did go on to heal the man physically. But He addressed his spiritual brokenness first.

The Greek word that we translate as 'save' is *sozo*. As well as meaning to save in the sense of rescuing from danger or destruction, *sozo* means to make well, to heal, to restore to health. Jesus is the great physician who saves us by healing our deep brokenness; this includes the whole of us – body, mind and spirit. Jesus came to make us whole again.

In his exegesis of Mark 4, Keller discusses the danger of building our lives around anything other than Jesus as the thing that will make us whole, whether that's success in a chosen career, healing from a physical condition or, as in my case, having a baby. As Keller says, when we do this, we make our wish into our saviour.[97] The problem is that the fulfilment of our wish or desire cannot possibly deliver all that we hope it will; only Jesus can do that.

These words hit me like a train; the setting and timing could not have been starker. There I was sitting in the fertility clinic at risk of doing exactly what Jesus teaches against – setting up my desire to have a baby as the thing that would sort my life out. That would mean the end of winter for us. I don't exaggerate when I say I felt like Jesus was sitting next to me in that waiting room using the words of Tim Keller to speak directly to me. I realised that so many of my prayers were requests for physical healing, to fix the physical problems that meant we were struggling to have babies. In my head, that was what I needed saving from – the things that were physically wrong with my body that were blocking my wish fulfilment. Just like the

---

[96] Timothy Keller, *King's Cross*, pp25-26.
[97] Timothy Keller, *King's Cross*, p28.

paralysed man, in that moment Jesus wasn't saying to me that I'd never have another baby or that IVF was not what we should be doing. He was simply saying, 'Don't focus on having a baby as the thing that will save you, the thing that will end winter. Instead, focus on Me.'

Counterfeit guides

It sounds harsh to our modern ears, but when we decide that the fulfilment of a particular desire is the thing that will make life complete and end our winter season, it becomes an idol. What is an idol? Today we might use this word in a positive way. In fact, the first definition of this word in the Oxford Learner's Dictionary is, 'a person or a thing that is loved and admired very much'.[98] We tend to use the term when thinking about inspirational people, those we aspire to be like. I've even heard children asked who their idols are.

But the biblical definition of an idol is much less favourable. It is a counterfeit god. An idol might promise all the same things as God, but the promises are hollow because the counterfeit god cannot deliver on the promises. For example, we might worship money because we believe the lie that if we had more money then we would feel complete, life would be better. So we work hard and earn more money, but it's never enough; we are never satisfied.

In my case, I set up motherhood as my saviour, the idea that being a mum would be the thing that would finally cure the ache in my soul. Since becoming a mum to Charlie, I have seen this for the lie it is. Don't get me wrong; motherhood is an immense privilege and blessing that brings joy and richness to my life in countless different ways. I am deeply grateful for Charlie and all he brings to our lives. But parenting is really, really hard. I am

[98] Definition of 'idol', Oxford Learner's Dictionary,
https://www.oxfordlearnersdictionaries.com/definition/english/idol
(accessed 13th November 2020).

regularly drawn up short by it. I have realised in new and various ways just how broken I am and how much I need the grace and mercy of God as I parent Charlie.

All that said, our desires are not wrong. For example, it wasn't wrong of me to want to have a family; it's not wrong to want to be good at what we do, or to meet someone we can share life with, or to be physically well. The problem is when these desires become disordered, when we worship these things rather than God, when we turn something good into something ultimate. As the apostle Paul articulates in Romans chapter 1, in our brokenness, humanity has 'exchanged the truth about God for a lie and worshipped and served the creature rather than the Creator' (Romans 1:25). We have set up counterfeit saviours when only Jesus can and does save us.

As well as not being able to save us, the Bible teaches that those who worship idols become like them:

> The idols of the nations are silver and gold,
> the work of human hands.
> They have mouths, but they do not speak;
> they have eyes, but they do not see;
> they have ears, but they do not hear,
> and there is no breath in their mouths.
> Those who make them
> and all who trust them
> shall become like them.
> *Psalm 135:15-18*

The truth is that we become like what we worship. If we worship God, we will become like Him, and because He is the source of life, we will become ever more fully alive. In stark contrast, if we worship counterfeit gods, we will become like them – lifeless.

Leaving home

In a previous chapter, I discussed Henri Nouwen's five lies of identity. In his writing, Nouwen goes on to explain how believing one or, in most of our cases, a combination of all of these lies about our identity leads to a sense of self-rejection. Our self-rejection manifests itself in one of two ways: either as low self-esteem, that sense that we will never be enough; or as pride, where we use our success, achievements, what we have, or the praise of others to over-inflate our sense of who we are. Both low self-esteem and pride are rejections of the true self because, rather than looking to God and His love to define us, we are relying on external circumstances to give us a sense of self.[99]

This sense of self-rejection coupled with a fundamental misunderstanding of who God is and a lack of trust in His goodness and love is the root of all our sin and, therefore, the cause of our brokenness. Why? Because it's this sense of self-rejection that leads us to worship counterfeit gods, to follow the wrong guides, if you like.

We end up following counterfeit guides who promise us an easier route to wholeness, to the fulfilment of our deepest desires. They promise to end our winter seasons. Ultimately, though, following these guides will leave us feeling exhausted and dissatisfied at a deep soul level because the promises of satisfaction they have made are hollow. All the routes they offer out of self-rejection never actually get us home; the fulfilment of our desires, home, lies forever just over the horizon.

Coming home

The Greek word *metanoia,* which is translated 'repent', literally means 'to change your mind'. Salvation involves a change of

---

[99] Henri J M Nouwen with Michael J Christensen and Rebecca J Laird, *Spiritual Direction*, pp30-31.

mind and a decision to go in a different direction. In chapter 15 of Luke's Gospel, Jesus tells a series of stories about lost things that the owners go out to search for: the lost sheep, the lost coin and the lost son. We are all lost. We are all the lost son. We have all left home in a futile attempt to satiate our heart's deepest desires for love, acceptance and security. The good news, literally 'the gospel', is that God, in Jesus, has come looking for us. God is scanning the horizon, looking for us to come home to the place where we are loved, valued and secure. Our role is simply to change our minds, to stop following our counterfeit guides and instead to choose to follow Jesus. He is the guide that we can trust to show us the way home because He knows the way.

Jesus' words from John 14, quoted at the beginning of this chapter, come in a profoundly intimate passage where Jesus talks about preparing a place in His Father's home for us (John 14:1-7). In first-century Jewish culture, before a couple got married, the bridegroom would build rooms onto his parents' house for him and his new wife to live in. In this passage, Jesus is likening himself to a loving bridegroom, preparing a room in His Father's home for His bride. He promises that, having built a room for us, He will show us the way home.

Coming home the hard way

The decision to stop following counterfeit guides and instead follow Jesus is not an easy one. In fact, in some ways it is likely to feel like dying because it is an act of surrender. We are surrendering to Jesus our sense of autonomy and control, our ability to choose our guides, and instead allowing Him to guide us. Like Jesus had to go through crucifixion to release new life, we too will go through our own crucifixions as we die to our false selves.

Choosing to follow Jesus rather than any other guide will also feel like dying because we are all in some ways addicted to our counterfeit guides. We believe their promises that they know the way out of self-rejection, that they know the way home. We believe them when they tell us that home lies just over the next hill. Being addicted to these things means that giving them up is hard; just ask any drug addict – going cold turkey feels like dying. But just like the seed that is planted doesn't die but is transformed, what looks like death is actually the birth of something new. When we die to our false selves, when we admit how lost we are and surrender to Jesus control for finding our way home, we find that the new life of our true selves is released.

This act of repentance, of choosing to follow Jesus, is not a one-time-only thing. On my own journey through winter, I found myself following counterfeit guides and, as a result, getting lost all the time. I had to decide to follow Jesus, to trust that He knew the way home, over and over again, often several times each day. I had to keep turning towards home.

Ultimately, just like for the paralysed man in the Gospel story at the beginning of this chapter, Jesus was gracious enough to give me what I had come asking for – a child. However, first He had to show me that, in my attempts to escape the sense of self-rejection, I had been following counterfeit guides. In the process, I had wandered far from home. I needed to realise the extent to which I was lost, and also that God in Jesus had come looking for me. I needed to know that I could come home, that my heavenly Father was longing for me to return home.

It's in the Father's house we find real love, acceptance and safety. In the Father's house, we can finally let go of the endless striving and searching of the false self and instead relax into our true, God-given identity. Here is where we find *shalom*, peace and wholeness. And Jesus is the only guide we can trust to lead us home.

Coming home, to God and to our true selves, is what will release new life in us, the new life of the Kingdom that is available to us no matter what the circumstances of our lives are. While we might be walking through a winter season of loss, it can be spring in our hearts as God births the new life of our true selves.

Walk it out

- Where in your life are you tempted to follow counterfeit guides?

- Perhaps you might like to do something physical to symbolise your repentance, your turning back to Jesus as your true guide. You might find it helpful to write down your counterfeit guides, the things you have relied on to get you home. Having done this, burn the paper to symbolise your decision to turn back to Jesus.

- Spend some time meditating on John 14:1-7. Picture Jesus preparing a room for you in the Father's house. How is it decorated and furnished? How does it feel to know there is a room prepared especially for you?

Provision for the pilgrim

If you then ... know how to give good gifts to your
children, how much more will your Father in heaven give
good things to those who ask him!

Matthew 7:11

During the coronavirus pandemic, there was a lot of discussion in the media about the effects the crisis had, and will continue to have, on people's mental well-being. As a result, there was also a lot of advice about how people could help to support their mental health. Suggestions included practising mindfulness and meditation, getting regular physical activity and spending less time on social media. All of these are very valid things which I wholeheartedly support and will unpack in the next section.

Yet, as community health psychologist Rochelle Burgess writes, 'A woman who has lost her job and cannot feed her family will find little relief from a meditation app.' She goes on to ask, 'Does a telephone counselling service connect people to food banks or charities that provide emergency shelter if they fear domestic violence? It should.' Burgess concludes the article with the truth that 'without food, shelter and safety, there can be little hope for sustaining good mental health during or after this crisis'.[100] Essentially, what the article is saying is that, when thinking about mental health, our approach needs to be holistic. You can't separate psychological needs from the physical necessities of life.

American psychologist Abraham Maslow articulated this in his 'hierarchy of needs'.[101] In this model, at the base of the pyramid are the basic human needs. Maslow called these the 'physiological needs'. These include the need for food, water, warmth and rest (sleep). On the next level up are the 'safety needs' – to feel safe and secure. It is only once these most basic of needs are met that we are in a position to focus on our psychological needs, which include the need for love and belonging and healthy self-esteem. Lastly, at the top of the pyramid are the self-fulfilment needs, such as achieving our full potential.

For the estimated 1.3 billion people around the world who live in poverty,[102] their entire lives can be consumed by trying to meet the most basic needs for food, water and shelter. Without meeting these needs, it is hard to speak of psychological needs such as love and belonging; these are just not the most pressing things.

During His earthly ministry, Jesus spoke about the Father's love for people. But, crucially, His actions also demonstrated that love, as He healed the sick and fed the hungry. God has always had a particular heart for the poor and marginalised. He is the 'Father of orphans and protector of widows' (Psalm 68:5).

---

[100] Rochelle Burgess, 'COVID-19 mental-health responses neglect social realities', 4 May 2020, https://www.nature.com/articles/d41586-020-01313-9 (accessed 13th November 2020).

[101] Abraham Maslow, *Motivation and Personality* (Harper, New York, 1954).

[102] According to a 2018 survey by the UN Development Program, 1.3 billion people live in what is termed 'multidimensional poverty'. While their income might be above the poverty line, they may have no access to electricity, clean water, a proper toilet or education. http://hdr.undp.org/en/2018-MPI (accessed 13th November 2020).

Without a father or husband to provide for them, these people would have been among the poorest in society.

More than this, God calls His people to demonstrate His love by caring for the poor and vulnerable. The people of Israel were commanded not to reap to the edges of their fields or go through their vineyards a second time. They were to leave some of the harvest for the poor (Leviticus 19:9-10). In the New Testament, when talking about the importance of putting our faith into action, the apostle James wrote:

> If a brother or sister is naked and lacks daily food, and one of you says to them, 'Go in peace; keep warm and eat your fill,' and yet you do not supply their bodily needs, what is the good of that?
> *James 2:15-16*

As Maslow's hierarchy of needs suggests, it is a hollow message to go to the poor and speak of God's love without helping to meet their most basic of needs.

God provides for the whole of us

Too often, when thinking about God and His love, we can fall into the trap of over-spiritualising things. We can take out of context Jesus' words to the devil when tempted in the wilderness that, 'One does not live by bread alone, but by every word that comes from the mouth of God' (Matthew 4:4). We can wrongly think that God is less concerned with our physical needs. However, Jesus' words are a direct quote from Deuteronomy 8. In this chapter, Moses is exhorting the Israelites not to forget the Lord once they enter the Promised Land. He reminds them that during their forty years in the wilderness, God fed them with manna and that their clothes did not wear out nor did their feet swell. The key is that Moses is telling them to remember who it was that provided for all their needs – God.

Jesus says the same thing on the Sermon on the Mount when He tells His followers not to worry about what they will wear, what they will eat or what they will drink, not because these things are not necessary, but because our heavenly Father knows we need them and will provide them for us (Matthew 6:25-34; Luke 12:22-31). Living this way leaves us free to 'strive first for the kingdom', in the knowledge that our loving heavenly Father will meet all our earthly needs.

During our winter season, I witnessed God provide for us in the most incredible ways. He provided a new home for us, amazing family and friends who loved us through our losses, and a new job for me.

A fresh start

When I fell pregnant with Libby, I was working for a paediatric research group at the University of Oxford. My role was to support consultants working in the Children's Hospital who wanted to undertake clinical research. Many of the research projects involved working with neonatal consultants who were caring for babies born prematurely. While this was important work, in the immediate aftermath of Libby's death, I knew that I would struggle to go back. It was all too close to our own experience. I couldn't spend my working life surrounded by babies whom the medical staff were doing all they could to keep alive.

In fact, before I even fell pregnant with Libby, I had felt God gently drawing me to something new. Many mornings on my drive into work, I had heard the gentle whisper of the Spirit saying, 'There's more than this.' It was for this reason that I had started my studies with WTC. I wanted to explore what the 'something more' might be.

Fast forward ten months from the start of my studies and I found myself staying in the bereavement flat at the John Radcliffe hospital in Oxford. It was a place I knew existed from my work with the neonatal department but hoped I'd never have to occupy. During our forty-eight-hour stay in this flat, Jon and I talked about what I might do workwise, as we both knew it wouldn't be what I had been doing. I vividly remember saying to Jon, 'I'd love to work for WTC as one of their Hub Directors.' The Hub Directors are the bridge between the central WTC office and the Hub communities that are formed at churches around the country. The role is varied, from recruiting students each year to supporting the existing student community to making sure that Hub evenings run smoothly. While both Jon and I could see how this would be a good fit for me, we had no idea how it could happen. As a result, the idea lay dormant for a year.

During this time, after six months of maternity leave, I returned to my work with the research group in Oxford. Something in me felt it was important to go back. Jon and I used to regularly talk about 'knocking skittles down', a skittle being something that was associated with painful memories. We didn't want to have 'no-go' places or people. For me, going back into the place I had worked before Libby died felt like a skittle I needed to knock down. That said, having gone back, I soon felt that God was releasing me. My decision to leave wasn't about running away; instead, it was about walking into something new that God had for me. Just a month after returning to work I resigned, having absolutely no clue what I was going to do!

It was something a very good friend said to me that helped me to jump. She said that often when God has something new that He wants to give us, we have to release what we are holding on to first. Saint Augustine said something similar when he wrote that 'God is always looking to give us good things but our hands are too full to receive them'.[103] When we open our hands and let something go there is a scary moment when our hands are empty, but this allows us to hold out our open hands to God, who then places something new and better into them.

[103] Quoted in Gerald G May, *Addiction and Grace: Love and Spirituality in the Healing of Addictions* (Harper Collins, New York, 1991), p17.

This is exactly how it was for me. I had three weeks when my hands were empty. I had released my current job but didn't know what would be next. During this time, I had my last Hub evening as a student with WTC. My Hub was based down in Winchester, and on my drive from Oxford to Winchester that evening I felt God remind me of the conversation I had had with Jon all those months earlier about how I'd love to be a Hub Director.

The Hub Director at the time, the wonderful Catherine Delve, had become a good friend to me over the months since Libby had died, and I would often meet her before a Hub evening for a catch-up; this evening was one of those times. As we sat down with cups of tea in hand, Catherine shared with me that she had been promoted to a role within WTC's Head Office. In the next breath, she said, 'Would you like my job here?'

In a heartbeat I replied, 'Yes please!'

And so, just a year after Libby was born, I found myself as the new Hub Director for the Hampshire Hub for WTC. It was a role I absolutely loved and thrived in. God had indeed put something new and better into my empty hands.

Enough is enough

When it comes to trusting in God's provision, there are two parts to our trust. Firstly, do we trust Him to provide at all? Secondly, do we trust that He will provide enough? The first of these is contingent upon the second. We will only fully trust God to provide if we believe that His provision will be sufficient to meet our needs

The problem is that we live in a culture that is endlessly striving for more. More possessions, more achievements and qualifications, more money, more memorable experiences, and so on. Walter Brueggemann argues that the problem with our culture of more is that it generates 'a restlessness that issues inescapably in anxiety'.[104] Brueggemann goes on to state that this restlessness and anxiety lead us to violence against each other as we compete for resources, and violence against creation as we consume too much of its natural resources.

When talking about needs, we must first acknowledge the difference between needs and desires. Too often we confuse our desires – what we want – with our needs. The cause of this confusion goes back to everything we have talked about regarding our broken sense of self. When we are alienated from our true selves, we find ourselves scrabbling to fill the hole that only God and His love can fill.

Prodigal God

Personally, what often stops me trusting in God to provide is the lie that, in some way, God's provision will be stingy or second-rate. I think, to be honest, I have been to too many Christian events with bad coffee and stale biscuits! In reality, nothing could be further from the truth. Ronald Rolheiser writes powerfully about how God is the 'absolute antithesis of everything that is stingy, miserly, frugal, narrowly calculating, or sparing in what it doles out. God is prodigal.' Rolheiser goes on to state that the dictionary definition of 'prodigal' is 'wastefully extravagant and lavishly abundant'.[105] We only have to look out at the created world to see God's lavish abundance and wasteful extravagance in operation. As David Benner has said, we have got the title of Jesus' famous parable about the wayward son wrong. Rather than being the story of the prodigal son, it's the story of the prodigal father, 'a man extravagantly lavish with his love'.[106] At its heart, the struggle to trust God and His provision

---

[104] Walter Brueggemann, *Sabbath as Resistance: Saying No to the Culture of Now* (Westminster John Knox Press, Louisville, 2014), p xii.
[105] Ronald Rolheiser, *Sacred Fire*, p277.
[106] David G Benner, *Surrender to Love*, p22.

comes down to the fight to believe that God is a good, loving Father who longs to give good gifts to His children.

I have experienced the prodigal way God provides, both in my life and also in the lives of others whom I love. For example, I have seen God provide financially in the most incredible way for someone I know when their marriage broke down. I termed it the economics of the Kingdom; my friend was better off than she had been before life fell apart. When God provides, He doesn't do it sparingly.

Asking instead of grasping

So much of what I'm writing in this book is me preaching to myself. I am a long way from having any of this sorted in my life, and this is definitely true when it comes to trusting in God's provision.

Recently I found myself in this place again. One day in my quiet time I felt drawn to spend some time reflecting on Jesus' words in Luke 12 where He says, 'Do not worry about your life, what you will eat, or about your body, what you will wear' (Luke 12:22). When I am living out of my false self, I am consumed by precisely these things. What am I doing with my life? What have I achieved? Are my clothes fashionable enough? All of this leads me to grasp for things to meet what I think are my needs. It leads me away from communion with God into self-sufficiency. I end up striving and pushing at work to prove myself. I buy more clothes in a futile attempt to make myself feel attractive enough.

In the quiet, a thought popped into my head. What would life look like if, instead of grasping for what I think I need, I started asking God to meet my needs? What if I were to trust in His abundant provision? The answer is that life would be more restful. I would feel more content, less anxious. I'd discover that my everyday concerns are met; God knows what I need in every area of my life. I can trust Him to provide for me, from the basic needs of food, shelter, water and rest to loving relationships and a sense of meaning and purpose in life. I might have less of what I think I need, but I would have everything I need. More than this, I'd experience more *shalom*, the peace and wholeness that Jesus promises us. I don't know about you, but I definitely need more of that in my life.

Mind the gap

Winter in nature is a season of scarcity, when the abundance of summer and autumn can feel like a distant memory. The same is true in our lives when we walk through winter seasons of loss. Everything is stripped back, and we can worry about how we will meet all our needs. For example, perhaps you have lost your job, and you now find yourself worrying about having enough money to provide for yourself or your family. Or maybe your marriage has fallen apart, and you find yourself as a single parent anxious about doing the best for your children.

During these times, it's fundamentally important that we don't develop a scarcity mentality that says, 'I don't know where the next bit of money or food will come from so I will scrabble hard to get as much as I can now and hoard it.' Thinking this way only leads to anxiety and often costs other people. Look at the chaos in our supermarkets that ensued just before the coronavirus lockdown. The phrase 'panic buying' is very apt; this is exactly what happened. People were anxious about the global situation and whether supply chains would be affected, so they stockpiled vast quantities of food (and toilet roll!). The result was empty shelves, and organisations such as food banks struggling to get the vital supplies they needed in order to care for the most vulnerable.

Jon is a dairy farmer and, on the farm, the solution to the scarcity of winter is to harvest crops in the summer. These crops are stored and then fed to the cows in the winter. Crucially, the cows neither store the crops nor provide for themselves; they simply turn up every day knowing that Jon and his staff will feed them. At the risk of comparing ourselves to cows, just like Jon provides daily for his cows in the wintertime, we can trust God to supply our 'daily bread' each and every day. We don't need to hoard or stockpile.

As I was writing this chapter, I wrestled with what the difference is between hoarding and wise stewardship. When I have used Jesus' words in Luke 12 as part of a group meditation, the objection I often hear is around not wanting to be people who don't work hard or steward resources wisely. I completely understand this concern, and I don't want to be that person either.

Here I find it helpful to think about the difference between having open or closed hands. If our motivation for wise stewardship is open-handed, where we see that all we have is not ours but a gift from God to us and our call is to steward this gift wisely, then we will still be able to be generous towards others. Hoarding looks like the closed fist. What lies behind this is often a sense of self-sufficiency – we have worked hard for this; we deserve it. Alternatively, it can be motivated by a scarcity mentality, the fear that there won't be enough to go around, or we will be left out. Crucially, the scarcity mentality means we are no longer in a place to be generous towards others as we are looking to our own interests.

There is another problem with the scarcity mentality. When we are focused on looking at the lack – what we don't have – we miss everything that we do have. We don't see how God has provided abundantly for us because we are focused on what's missing. This is something that God spoke to me powerfully about on Libby's last birthday.

As you can imagine, Libby's birthdays are tough times when the black hole of grief opens up to consume much more of life than normal. One of the things that I like to do on her birthday is to take a quiet walk. It was during this walk last year that I felt God gently encourage me not to live in a scarcity mentality. As I thought about this, I realised that over the preceding few days I had lived in a place of lack rather than abundance. We were on a family holiday, and at times like these I find myself feeling bad for Charlie that he doesn't have any siblings with him. I find myself thinking and saying things like, 'He shouldn't be on his own,' or, 'It was never my intention to have an only child; Charlie should have his sister with him.' The problem with thinking this way is that there are so many ways things could have turned out. Who knows what would have happened if Libby had lived? Jon and I might have decided not to have any more children after her, or we might have waited a while longer. It is not a foregone conclusion that Charlie would be here. When I inhabit a scarcity mentality, rather than focusing on all that is good and how blessed we are to have Charlie, I just see what we are missing.

As I thought about this, I felt prompted to sit and open my hands as a gesture of release, of letting Libby go again, trusting that she is safe with Jesus, that I will one day meet her and know her. Letting go helped me to step out of the anxiety and pain of scarcity and into the joy and gratitude that flows when I recognise God's abundant provision in my life.

When life falls apart and we are tempted to grasp for or hoard the things we think we need, there is another way. Rather than grasping, we can instead open our hands to our loving Father, release the things we have been holding on to that are not His best for us, and ask Him for his provision. We can choose to trust that He will provide all we need out of the lavish abundance of His love for us.

Walk it out

- What do you need God to provide for you so that you can keep walking through your winter season? You might find it helpful to write down your needs.

- Is there something you feel God is asking you to let go of that is blocking either His provision in your life or stopping you from seeing how He has already provided for you? Perhaps you could spend some time in prayer with your hands open to symbolise both your release of these things and your willingness to receive the good gifts God has for you.

- If you resonate with the concept of grasping for things or struggle with anxiety and worry, spend some time meditating on Matthew 6:25-34. Journal anything you feel God say to you.

Walk your own path

Let's just go ahead and be what we were made to be,
without enviously or pridefully comparing ourselves with
each other, or trying to be something we aren't.

Romans 12:6 (*The Message*)

Probably like many of you, during the coronavirus pandemic I had to become much more familiar than I would want to be with videoconferencing apps such as Zoom. This technology was an incredible gift during the season of coronavirus lockdowns. It meant that families and friends could remain connected; it allowed churches to broadcast live straight into people's homes; it enabled many millions of people to work from home and still be connected with their colleagues. While we had to isolate physically, we weren't isolated socially.

One of the things that the reliance on videoconferencing, coupled with everyone being at home, did was to give us a look inside people's homes, from the people that we work with to other parents in our child's class, and even into the homes of the rich and famous. It became a running joke between Jon and me that if you want to be taken seriously on video calls, you really need impressively full bookshelves behind you.

I am prone to comparison with others, if I'm honest; it is my Achilles heel. Being able to see into other people's homes didn't help this. I found myself comparing my home with other people's. Did I have enough books on my bookshelves? Was my home stylish enough? Or simply, gosh I wish my house was as tidy as theirs. I rarely came out well from this process.

I often talk with people about the tyranny of the 'oughts' and 'shoulds'. When we spend our lives comparing ourselves, we find ourselves using these words a lot. For example, at the beginning of the coronavirus lockdown, I was barely managing to look after Charlie full-time, let alone keep on top of all the cooking, cleaning and washing. However, I would torment myself by thinking about all the people who seemed to be breezing through it all, like the parents who seemed to have homeschooling nailed. Or the people who had the most immaculate homes (at least the part they chose to show me on Zoom). Or the friends who were using the time to engage in creative projects or volunteer in their local communities.

Thinking this way launched an internal torrent of 'shoulds' and 'oughts'. I 'should' be able to teach my five-year-old without both of us having to have regular moments on the time-out step (for me, this meant hiding in the toilet!). I 'ought' to be using this time to develop new and delicious recipes for my family. When I was in the spiral of comparison, I missed all the nuggets of joy that this time gave us because, as Theodore Roosevelt famously said, 'Comparison is the thief of joy.'

I wish I was like you

The other problem with comparisons is that we are always comparing our 'backstage' to other people's 'front stage'. Take Zoom calls as an example. Here we are only shown what that person has chosen to show us. We don't know what the rest of their home looks like. But we do know what our home looks like. We're not comparing like for like. The same is true for all social media – we are only seeing what people choose to show us.

When Jon and I were in the midst of our winter season, I found it very hard to be out among couples with babies. This turned innocuous places like the local shopping centre into a minefield. Why is it that when we are struggling with a gaping hole in our lives, it appears that we are surrounded by people who have what we desperately desire? For me, the world seemed full of heavily pregnant women or people with babies. For you, it might be loved-up couples, or happy families where both parents are around, and everything looks perfect. Or maybe it's other people's children who don't have the learning disability your child has, or people who don't live in chronic pain. Or the couple who have the perfect home, or people who have their 'dream job' – there are so many different blanks you could fill in here.

I vividly remember one weekend when Jon and I were walking through a large department store, and yet again it felt that couples with prams were everywhere. I was slipping into a 'compare–despair' hole as I enviously watched yet another pram occupied by yet another cute little baby, pushed by yet another pair of adoring parents. It was then I felt the Spirit gently say to me, 'You have no idea what that couple's personal situation is, what it might have taken for them to have that baby, or what else might be going on in their lives.' I have to say that stopped me in my tracks. I was reminded of this several years later when we finally got to be the proud couple pushing our baby through the same shop. There may well have been people looking enviously on that day, not knowing what we had walked through to get to that point.

Much like cancer can spread through a body and kill, comparison if left unchecked can spread to every area of our lives, killing us from the inside out. Constantly comparing ourselves with others leaves us restless and discontented. Whether it's that someone has a tidier home than we do, is more accomplished in their work than we are, has better-behaved children than we do, is more 'spiritual' than we are – whatever it is, the comparison only leads one way: to despair. Comparison leads us into the black hole of self-rejection. Comparison confirms our internal bias that we are not enough as we are. It takes us away from home and blocks the flow of God's love in our lives. Comparison takes us away from our true self into the false self. Here, as a result of the 'oughts' and 'shoulds', we often end up desperately trying to be something we're not.

I'm glad I'm not you

While we can probably all see that what psychologists term 'upward social comparison' is generally unhealthy, what about its opposite, 'downward social comparison'? What about comparing ourselves to those who don't have all that we have or are in a more challenging situation than us. Is this ever a good thing? Research has suggested that, in certain circumstances, the answer to this question is yes. To use a relatively trivial example, I know I can feel better about myself if I believe I know more about a particular topic than someone else. Or what about the times when our child is better behaved than someone else's?

On a more serious note, downward social comparison is something that we all use when we're going through tough times. I'm sure we've all had conversations with friends or family members who are going through a tough time and, to try to pull themselves together, they'll say something along the lines of, 'Well, it could be worse... look at what so-and-so is going through.' In this situation, we could argue that downward comparison helps. Why? Because it can help us find perspective in our own situation, to find the moments of joy and goodness. It helps us to be grateful for all that we do have rather than focusing on what we don't have.

To my mind, however, using the darkness of others to find the light in my situation is not a good place to be. What's more, I know from experience that this strategy doesn't always work.

Compare – despair

The truth is, comparison of suffering is never going to aid us on our journey through winter because it leads to despair. Rather than helping us to make the best of our situation, comparison can either lead to self-pity or a victim mentality – in a sense, a kind of inverted pride that our circumstances are much worse than other people's – or it can make us feel guilty about how we feel because someone else's problems are much worse than ours. Comparison with others keeps us in the darkness of despair, either feeling that no one has it as bad as we do or feeling the pain of the darkness of others.

What is the opposite of despair? Hope. It is hope that will light up the darkness of winter. It is hope that will take away the chill. It is hope that will calm the storms. It is hope that will give us the perseverance to keep walking when it gets hard. Where does hope come from? It comes from God who is the God of hope (Romans 15:13). Rather than comparing our pain with others, we need to stay connected to our source of hope.

What follow in the rest of this book are my strategies for doing just that. They are practices that I found helpful when walking through winter as they kept me focused on following Jesus and so helped me to be hopeful amid the heartache.

Walk it out

- Have you ever used comparison as a means to help you to feel better about a tough situation that you are walking through? Why did you do this? Did it help?

- Does the idea that comparison only leads to despair and takes us into our false selves resonate with you? When have you seen this in your own life? You might want to journal your response to this question.

- Spend some time meditating on *The Message* Translation of Romans 12:6.

Part 4

Hygge for the Heartbroken

As the Father has loved me, so I have loved you; abide in

my love.

John 15:9

Hygge

'They're getting hygge,' ... 'Sorry, what?'

Helen Russell[107]

A couple of years ago, I read British journalist and author Helen Russell's book, *The Year of Living Danishly*. In this book, Helen tells the story of her and her husband's move to Denmark for her husband's work at the Lego headquarters. Charlie is just discovering Lego, and I think at the moment this would be his dream job.

As a journalist, Helen decides to spend her time researching why Denmark consistently ranks among the top ten happiest nations. Danes are the happiest people in Europe, according to the European Social Survey;[108] this is despite experiencing long, cold, dark winters.

Helen and 'Lego Man' (as she affectionately calls her husband) arrive in Denmark in January. It's freezing cold and dark, and the streets are deserted. When she asks cultural integration coach (yes, that is a job!) Pernille Chaggar where everyone is, Pernille's response is, 'They're getting *hygge*.'[109] Understandably, Helen has no idea even how to pronounce *hygge*

---

[107] Helen Russell, *The Year of Living Danishly: Uncovering the Secrets of the World's Happiest Country* (Icon Books, 2015, accessed from Scribd (www.scribd.com)), p38.

[108] Meik Wiking, *The Little Book of Hygge*, p9.

[109] Helen Russell, *The Year of Living Danishly*, p38.

(in case you're wondering, it's pronounced hoo-guh), much less what it means. Actually, *hygge* isn't easy to explain, but essentially, it's about getting cosy.

Happiness researcher Meik Wiking writes, 'The word *"hygge"* originates from a Norwegian word meaning "well-being".'[110] Central to *hygge* are feelings of being loved, warm and safe. While happiness is multi-factorial, *hygge* appears to play an important part in why Danes are among the happiest people in the world. Through practising *hygge*, Danes don't endure winter; they embrace it. It is for this reason that I think *hygge* has something to teach us as we walk through winter seasons of loss.

So, what are the essential ingredients of *hygge*? There are many elements to it, but central to them all is home. While pubs, cafes and restaurants can be *hyggelig* (cosy), the best place to practice *hygge* is in your home. This is why the streets were deserted when Helen arrived in Denmark in January; everyone was at home getting *hyggelig*. Light comes next, particularly candlelight. The Danes burn more candles per head than any other country in the world.[111]

Crucially, while you can practise *hygge* on your own, in Denmark it mostly happens in small groups of close friends or family. What's more, the work of *hygge* is shared by all. It's not left up to the host to do all the work; the load is shared, with everyone pitching in to help. Comfort food is an important ingredient of *hygge*. Play is also essential. Finally, presence and gratitude are important – being fully present to the moment and to others and being grateful for what we have rather than looking at what we don't have.[112]

In what follows, I have created what I call '*hygge* for the heartbroken'. These are practices that can help us experience love, warmth and a sense of security as we walk through winter. These practices have the same essential ingredients as *hygge*:

---

[110] Meik Wiking, *The Little Book of Hygge*, p9.

[111] Meik Wiking, *The Little Book of Hygge*, p9.

[112] Meik Wiking, *The Little Book of Hygge*, pp46-47.

home, light, close relationships, good food, gratitude, rest and hospitality. These practices can help us to embrace rather than endure winter. They can help us hold on to hope in the middle of the heartbreak and hold joy and sorrow together.

Home

One thing I asked of the LORD,

that I will seek after:

to live in the house of the LORD

all the days of my life.

Psalm 27:4

What do you think of when you think of home? For me, words like refuge, acceptance, belonging, love, family, warmth and safety come to mind. Home is a shelter from the storms of both nature and life. One of the things I love about winter is curling up in bed with a good book and listening to a storm rage outside. I realise that I'm fortunate that home has such positive connotations. I know that's not the case for everyone.

We talked in an earlier chapter about how our loving heavenly Father is always inviting us home: home to His love and acceptance, home to our true selves. The Father's house is the ultimate place of safety. It's the place where we truly belong. When we're walking through winter seasons of loss, the Father's house is the place in which we need to dwell to help guard against the cold and dark of winter. The Father's house is a place of refuge from the elements of winter.

Home is where the heart is

Home is where our hearts are. It's where we love and are loved. So it follows that the way to make sure we stay at home in the Father's house as we walk through winter is to look at where our hearts are. If we want to dwell in God's house, we have to direct our hearts, our love, towards God. Our hearts need to be at home with God.

Attention is the beginning of devotion

If we want to know where our hearts are, we need to look at what we are spending our time on, what we are giving our attention to. Why? Because, as pastor and author John Mark Comer articulates, attention leads to awareness.[113] When we turn our attention to God, we become aware of His love, His goodness and His grace – in short, His presence with us. When it feels like God is absent, He is not the one who has wandered; we are. When we turn our attention back to God, our hearts come home to Him.

In today's world, there are so many things that vie for our attention: twenty-four-hour news, social media, Netflix, YouTube, emails and books. That's not even to mention our work and relational commitments. We live in an age of information overload. In his 1982 book *The Critical Path*, futurist Buckminster Fuller estimated how long it took for knowledge from the time of birth of Jesus (AD 0) to double in size. His estimate was about 1,500 years. Now, with the advent of the internet, it is estimated that rather than taking centuries, knowledge doubles every twelve hours![114] Is it any

---

[113] John Mark Comer, *The Ruthless Elimination of Hurry: How to Stay Emotionally Healthy and Spiritually Alive in the Chaos of the Modern World* (Hodder & Stoughton, London, 2019), pp53-54.
[114] 'Rapid Doubling of Knowledge Drives Change in How We Learn', Float, 23 January 2018, https://gowithfloat.com/2018/01/rapid-

wonder that many of us feel overwhelmed and as though we are drowning in a sea of information? Combine this with the wisdom that says being well *informed* is not the same as being well *formed*, and we can see we have a problem![115]

Being kept in between

In the immediate aftermath of Libby's death, I spent a lot of time watching rubbish TV and reading trashy novels. I was trying to 'zone out' and escape the reality of what we were facing. To be honest, part of this was just that I was not yet in a place where I could start to acknowledge the grief that I was feeling. In terms of the Kübler Ross cycle of grief, I was most definitely in denial and desperately trying to numb the pain. I turned to anything that would help me forget or continue to deny the pain. I remember night after night after Libby died pouring myself one too many glasses of wine and 'vegging out' in front of the London Olympic Games.

Another word for this is escapism. So much of the entertainment industry is geared around helping us to try to escape the reality of life. As Henri Nouwen points out, the literal meaning of the word entertainment is 'to keep someone in between'.[116]

Entertainment, whether that's in the form of television, cinema, computer games, books or hedonistic parties, keeps us 'somewhere in between', in a kind of 'no man's land'. As any soldier will tell you, in a battle situation, you don't want to spend too long in no man's land as it's the place where people die.

---

doubling-knowledge-drives-change-learn/ (accessed 19th November 2020).

[115] There is so much more I could say here regarding the problem of distraction when it comes to our spiritual formation. For a brilliant unpacking of all the issues I recommend Part 1 of John Mark Comer's book, *The Ruthless Elimination of Hurry*.

[116] Henri J M Nouwen, *Can You Drink the Cup?* (Ave Maria Press, 2006, accessed from Scribd (www.scribd.com)), p103.

While entertainment might not kill your physical body, it can definitely kill your soul.

Please don't misunderstand me. I am not saying that entertainment and having fun is a bad thing. I am not a finger-wagging puritan telling people that under no circumstances are they to have any fun! No. I am a firm believer in the importance of fun and, in particular, maintaining a sense of humour in the midst of pain. What I am saying is that we can't use entertainment as our refuge from the cold and dark of winter. Entertainment is not home; it is no man's land.

So how do we redirect our attention to God? How do we make sure we dwell in God's house as we walk through winter? The answer lies in being intentional with our attention.

Abiding with Jesus

In his book *The Common Rule*, corporate lawyer and author Justin Whitmel Earley unpacks the importance of intentionality when it comes to our habits.[117] He makes the point that we all have habits. If you doubt this, take an inventory of your life for a week and you'll see the habits emerge. After reaching burnout, Justin decided to begin to live more intentionally, creating habits that would help him to love God and love others better. He created a Rule of Life.

In our culture, and also in the charismatic church, we tend to recoil from the word 'rule'. We don't like anything that looks like it's going to limit our freedom; after all, we live in a culture that wants to believe we can live without limits.[118] In the Church, we recoil from the word 'rule' because it sounds too

---

[117] Justin Whitmel Earley, *The Common Rule: Habits of Purpose for an Age of Distraction* (InterVarsity Press, Downers Grove, 2019).
[118] However, it's interesting to note the popularity of books like Jordan B Peterson's *Twelve Rules for Life*. Might we be beginning to acknowledge the lie that freedom is found in living life without boundaries?

much like the religiosity and legalism that Jesus Himself taught against.

But we are getting the wrong end of the stick if we think of a Rule of Life as something legalistic. It's crucial to see that it is 'rule', not 'rules'. As Peter Scazzero explains in his book *Emotionally Healthy Spirituality*, the word 'rule' comes from the Greek for 'trellis'.[119] Think for a moment about a trellis in a garden: what does it do? By giving a structure for a plant to grow against, it helps the plant to grow upward towards the light. If I were to plant a climbing rose, I could leave it to grow by itself, and it would, but it would grow and climb much better if it had a trellis to grow up.

Essentially, a Rule of Life is a way of helping us to grow towards the light. It is a tool that can help us grow more fully into our true selves, to grow in our experience and awareness of God's love for us. From this foundation, we can go out and love others well. A Rule of Life will help us come home to God and to live from this place as we walk through winter seasons. A Rule of Life will help us to abide in Jesus (John 15:1-11). It will help us to make our home with Jesus. As we do this, He promises to make His home in us (John 14:23). What's more, if we abide in Jesus, we will bear fruit, no matter what the season.

One rule for one...

For our wedding anniversary this year, Jon and I had the most lovely twenty-four hours away at a local vineyard. As we walked through the vines, I realised that not every trellis was the same. There were different kinds of trellis for different varieties of grape. The same is true of a Rule of Life. The trellis that works for me and helps me to abide with Jesus and aids my growth

---

[119] Peter Scazzero, *Emotionally Healthy Spirituality: It's Impossible to Be Spiritually Mature While Remaining Emotionally Immature* (Zondervan, Grand Rapids, 2014), p190.

might not be what will help you. What's more, different seasons of life will require that we adapt our Rule of Life.

Just as the central element to *hygge* is the home, and it is the comfort and refuge of the home that helps Danes embrace winter, making our home with Jesus is what will help us to stay aware of God's presence with us despite the cold and dark of winter. It is an awareness of His presence that will help us to walk on through winter.

Walk it out

- What is your gut reaction to the idea of a Rule of Life? Does this seem inviting or restrictive?

- You might find it helpful to understand that we all have habits that are forming us – for good or bad. Before thinking about creating your own Rule of Life, you might like to take an 'inventory' of your current habits. Maybe take a week and log everything you do in those days.

- Spend some time reflecting on Jesus' invitation to abide in Him in John 15:1-11.

Gratitude

Give thanks in all circumstances; for this is the will of God

in Christ Jesus for you.

1 Thessalonians 5:18

If you were to ask Jon or any of my family members, they would all confirm that I am a bookworm. I love books, and I often have to smuggle packages into the house before Jon sees. Currently, I am blaming writing this book for the number of parcels that get delivered, but I won't be able to lean on this excuse forever!

While I read a lot, I can genuinely say that there are only a handful of books that have changed the way I live my life. Ann Voskamp's book, *One Thousand Gifts*, is one of them.[120] In this book, Ann talks about being dared by a friend to write a list of one thousand things for which she is thankful. She talks powerfully about how this has helped her to live life in the moment and to experience joy amid everyday life that is full of deadlines, debt, drama and mundane daily tasks.

Of course, Ann Voskamp is not the only person to link practising gratitude with happiness. Shawn Achor is a researcher in positive psychology, and the central premise of his work is

---

[120] Ann Voskamp, *One Thousand Gifts: A Dare to Live Fully Right Where You Are* (Zondervan, Grand Rapids, 2011).

that success doesn't breed happiness; rather, happiness breeds success. Through his research, Shawn has found that people who are happier and more content with life tend to be more successful. He has identified four habits that are regularly practised by happier people, and the first of these habits is gratitude. So practising gratitude is clearly important when it comes to thriving in life and cultivating a sense of well-being.[121]

The practice of gratitude is also rooted in Scripture. Throughout the Psalms, we find the exhortation to 'give thanks' to the Lord (Psalms 100; 107; 118). What's more, the apostle Paul teaches us that our prayer requests should be combined with thanksgiving: 'Do not worry about anything, but in everything by prayer and supplication with thanksgiving let your requests be made known to God' (Philippians 4:6). I can so often make the mistake of forgetting the thanksgiving part of prayer and instead just go straight to the 'shopping lists' of things I want God to do.

It's not just in the good times that the Bible tells us we should practise gratitude; as the verse quoted at the beginning of this chapter teaches, we are to 'give thanks in all circumstances' (1 Thessalonians 5:18). Notice Paul doesn't say that we should give thanks *for* all circumstances but *in* all circumstances. In the midst of really challenging circumstances like the loss of a loved one, a job or our health, it can be really hard to be thankful.

About six weeks after Libby died, I went on a retreat day. As part of this day, the lady leading the retreat asked us to spend some time journalling all the things for which we were thankful. Only once we had done this could we write a list of all the unmet desires of our hearts or the things that were causing us pain. I struggled with the idea of writing a gratitude list at that point in my journey through loss and spent a lot of time arguing with God about how I couldn't possibly do it. But then, slowly, I

---

[121] For more on this see Shawn's TED Talk, "The Happy Secret to Better Work',
https://www.ted.com/talks/shawn_achor_the_happy_secret_to_better_work (accessed 30th October 2020).

started to write my list. As I wrote, I realised just how much I still had to be thankful to God for. Writing my list of gratitudes led to a really powerful encounter with God, where my perspective changed, and I experienced joy despite the circumstances I found myself in.

Cultivating an 'attitude of gratitude' is essential when it comes to walking through the winter seasons of life. Through practising gratitude, we move our focus away from the problem, from the scarcity and lack, and instead focus on all we do have. It isn't about trying to ignore or gloss over the pain of tragedy and loss in life or the things that are not as we would want them to be. Instead, it's about refusing to let these things dominate. Practising gratitude will lead us to experience God's love and grace afresh in our lives, and this leads to a sense of joy that lights up the darkness of any situation in which we might find ourselves.

Grace recognised

Ann Voskamp makes this point very powerfully in her book when she talks about the Greek word used in the Bible that we translate 'to give thanks'. This word is *eucharisteo*, and it is the word used by Jesus in the Gospel descriptions of the Last Supper: 'Then he took a loaf of bread, and when he had given thanks, he broke it and gave it to them' (Luke 22:19). *Eucharisteo* is the word from which we get 'Eucharist', which is the Christian ceremony that commemorates the Last Supper. Ann goes on to explain that the Greek word for grace is *charis*, which is contained within the word *eucharisteo*. What's more, the Greek word for joy (*chara*) is derived from *charis*. So, in the one word, *eucharisteo*, we find thanksgiving, grace and joy.[122]

I hope you will forgive me for a little more Greek word study. One of the cognate nouns of *chara* (joy) is *xara*, which means 'an awareness of God's grace, favour and joy', or 'grace

---

[122] Ann Voskamp, *One Thousand Gifts*, pp30-32.

recognised'. I love this idea that joy is 'grace recognised', a renewed awareness that God is always leaning towards us in love.

It is for this reason that gratitude is the first of our *hygge* practices. I like to think of gratitude as the front door key that opens the way for us to enter into God's house. Gratitude is the key to unlocking joy, a joy we can experience no matter what we are going through in life because the source of this joy is not the circumstances of life but God. Joy comes from knowing that God's grace and mercy follow us all the days of our lives. As King David said, knowing this allows us to 'dwell in the house of the LORD [our] whole life long' (Psalm 23:6).

After I read Ann's book, I started a gratitude journal. It was about a year after Libby died and we were still very much in the middle of our winter season. We had lost another baby through miscarriage, and life was tough. It was very easy to focus on all that I didn't have or had lost. However, at the end of each day, I would write down at least three things for which I was grateful. The stuff I journalled ranged from little things like a good cup of coffee to the bigger things of life like being thankful for God's love and presence with me that day, or the love of my husband, family and friends.

This daily practice helped me to see the beauty in the midst of all the pain. I would talk with my friends about hunting for the nuggets of gold in my day. Just as there is beauty to be found in the natural world in the middle of winter, from the sparkling, glistening glory of a frosty morning or the delicate, unique intricacy of a snowflake or the joy of snuggling up beside a warm fire, there is beauty to be found in the middle of our winter season of loss.

Walk it out

- If you don't already have one, go out and buy yourself a journal specifically for writing daily gratitudes.

- Each day (I tend to do mine at night-time), write at least three things for which you are thankful (research says the optimum number is eight). Try not to repeat yourself or make them too extraordinary. Regularly review your gratitude journal and write about how it makes you feel to read through them all.

- You might like to spend some time meditating on James 1:17: 'Every generous act of giving, with every perfect gift, is from above, coming down from the Father of lights.'

Light

Your word is a lamp to my feet

and a light to my path.

Psalm 119:105

I'm sure we all remember the old playground rhyme, 'Sticks and stones may break my bones, but words will never hurt me.' I know I used it at school to try to fend off the class bully. The problem is, it isn't true. Words can and do hurt, and often cause far more lasting damage than a stick or a stone might. Words are powerful; they have the power to build up and the power to tear down. The apostle James writes about the power of words when he says, 'A word out of your mouth may seem of no account, but it can accomplish nearly anything – or destroy it … By our speech we can ruin the world, turn harmony to chaos, throw mud on a reputation' (James 3:5-6, *The Message*). Other passages in the Bible go so far as to say, 'Words kill, words give life; they're either poison or fruit – you choose' (Proverbs 18:21, *The Message*). As we walk through winter, words can either light up the darkness and so bring life, or they can take us further into the darkness of despair.

Life-giving words

The power of words to light up the darkness is affirmed from the very first page of the Bible. In fact, God's first words are, 'Let there be light' (Genesis 1:3). It is hugely significant that in the Genesis account of creation, God creates using words. Throughout the creation account, we read, 'And God said ...' This account of creation affirms not only the creative power of words but also the creative power of God. In many ways, Genesis 1 is an attack (a polemic) on other Ancient Near Eastern (ANE) creation myths that the original readers would have been well aware of. For example, the Babylonian Enuma Elish describes how the world was created through a violent and bloody battle between competing gods. Within this myth, humanity is created to serve the gods. Contrast this with Genesis where we see God create, not through violence or any physical act but simply through His speech. God speaks, and it happens. What's more, in the Genesis account, God creates humanity in His image. Not to serve Him but to rule and reign with Him. The Genesis account makes some very bold statements about who God is and also who we are.[123]

The power of God's words to bring life is also seen throughout the Gospel accounts of Jesus' earthly ministry. The apostle John tells us at the beginning of his Gospel that Jesus is the word of God. The biblical scholar F F Bruce argues that the translation of the original Greek word *logos* to 'word' is inadequate when it comes to helping us understand what the apostle John is trying to say. Bruce suggests that to help us, we need to understand that in the Old Testament 'the "word of God" denotes God in action, especially in creation, revelation and deliverance'.[124] Jesus is 'God in action'. Throughout Jesus' earthly ministry, we see the 'word of God' in action, healing the sick, calming storms, releasing the demon-possessed.

---

[123] For more on this see J Richard Middleton, *The Liberating Image*.
[124] F F Bruce, *The Gospel of John*, p64.

In Genesis 1 we read that God's words light up the darkness and create life; in John's Gospel we see the 'word of God' re-creating life; we see the 'light of the world' (John 8:12) bringing new life and deliverance to those trapped in the bondage and darkness of death.

Death-dealing words

The enemy knows too the power of words to bring light and life. Contrast the life-giving words of God in Genesis 1 with Genesis 3. Here the serpent uses words to bring the darkness of death when he plants in Eve's mind a seed of doubt about God's goodness and trustworthiness. The serpent suggests to Eve that God does not have her best interests at heart and that she and Adam can be like God by eating the fruit. What is the result? Humanity is cut off from God, and because God is the source of life, this leads only one way – to death. Adam and Eve are expelled from the garden to live a life of striving and hustle. A life lived from the false self rather than the true self.

Blessings and curses

It may sound harsh to our modern ears but, given the power of words to create life or to tear it down, the biblical writers tell us that words are either blessings or curses. In the Bible, blessings bring life. It's the blessing of God that causes the creatures of the earth to be fruitful and multiply. In contrast, curses lead to death.

As a result of the power of words to bring life or lead to death, earlier in his letter the apostle James teaches that just like the rudder can set the course of a ship, while it might be small, the tongue can set the course of our whole lives (James 3:4-5). We need to be really careful about the words that come out of our mouths; this is important no matter what the circumstances of our lives, but especially so when we are walking through winter seasons. We need to speak words of light and life, of blessing over ourselves and our situation.

Words are a weapon

When we were walking through our winter season, I often felt like I was in a battle. In many ways I was. This wasn't a physical battle; it was a battle for hope, and my life was most definitely on the line. At times this was my physical life as I contemplated escape through suicide. But always, what was at stake was the life of my true self – my God-given identity. I had a choice to make. Would I listen to the death-dealing words of the enemy and either give in to the darkness of despair or attempt to fix the situation myself? Or would I instead choose words of life, which would help me to light up the darkness and find hope, meaning and purpose amid the heartache and pain?

As always, Jesus is our model. How does Jesus come against the devil when tempted to live from His false self? With words. Crucially, the words of Scripture (see Matthew 4:1-11). The apostle Paul affirms the power of words in our battles in his famous description of the armour of God (Ephesians 6:13-17). Significantly, the only weapon of attack, of offence, is the sword of the Spirit. What is the sword of the Spirit? It is the word of God.

One of the most important ways we can light up the darkness of our winter season with hope is through meditating on the Bible. In her book *The Disciple*, theologian and WTC Principal Lucy Peppiatt writes about the importance of memorising Scripture.[125] Just like a sword stowed in the belt of a solider, if we can commit to memory some key Bible verses and passages, we will have them ready to hand when we need them.

---

[125] Lucy Peppiatt, *The Disciple: On Becoming Truly Human* (Cascade Books, Eugene, 2012), p51.

I have to admit that I have never found it easy to memorise whole passages of the Bible. What I have tended to do, and what I did in the days and weeks after Libby died, was to have sticky notes around the house with Bible verses on them. When I was struggling with the darkness of the situation, I would turn to these verses to find the light of God's love. I had verses that reminded me of the promise of His presence, like Psalm 34:18: 'The LORD is near to the broken-hearted, and saves the crushed in spirit.' Or Jesus' final words to the disciples in Matthew 28:20: 'And remember, I am with you always, to the end of the age.' I also had verses that gave me hope for restoration, such as Psalm 30:5: 'Weeping may linger for the night, but joy comes with the morning.' I also loved God's words to the people of Judah that He would repay them the years that the locusts had eaten (Joel 2:25). These little sticky notes were like little tea lights that helped me to light up the darkness.

Learning to love liturgy

In the days immediately after Libby died, my mum was staying with my uncle and his wife, who live not too far from us. Every day during this period, Mum attended Morning Prayer services at the local church. As a result, she encouraged me to use the Anglican Liturgy for Morning Prayer. This was not a form of prayer and worship that I was familiar with and, to be honest, I had always tried to steer clear of liturgical services. But when I didn't know where to start in terms of praying or reading the Bible, using this liturgical form of worship gave structure and form to both my reading of the Bible and, crucially, my prayers.

The words of liturgical services are beautiful and true; they are words of light and life. As such, they are a powerful weapon when it comes to lighting up the darkness of our winter seasons. For example, when I didn't know what to pray after Libby died, reciting the Lord's Prayer each day as part of my morning worship was hugely powerful.

Engaging with liturgy has changed the way I pray. Now when I am asked to pray for someone, invariably I will start by praying the Lord's prayer over them. I can't think of better words to use than the ones that Jesus Himself gave us.

More than this, I love the fact that when I use the liturgy, I am joining with other people around the world who are all using the same form of words to worship God. There is something hugely powerful about the fact that, while I might be sitting on my own engaging with the words of Morning Prayer or Compline, I am not alone; I am part of a global community of faith.

Praise in the pain

I come from a family of music lovers. I have fond memories of family holidays driving down through France with the music on loud and all of us singing along. I am always amazed that it can be years since I last heard a song from one of our family trips, but yet, when it comes on the radio, I still know all the words. Sadly, as Dad often got to choose what we listened to, I know all the words to most Chris de Burgh and Cher songs. So not cool, I know.

On a serious point, though, the same is true of many of the worship songs that I regularly sing in church. While I might not be able to quote vast chunks of the Bible, I do know the words to my favourite worship songs, which only serves to highlight the importance of sound theology when it comes to the songs we sing. I have mentioned this before, but I think it bears repeating: as Tom Wright says, we learn 'a fair amount of our theology through the hymns we sing'.[126] When we think about the power of words and also about the fact that the ways we think about God influence how we face our winter seasons, we can see that the worship songs we sing week in week out must

---

[126] N T Wright, *For All the Saints? Remembering the Christian Departed* (SPCK, London, 2011), p xiv.

be biblically based and theologically sound. The words need to be true.

I love sung worship, and it has always been one of the main ways by which I engage with God and sense His presence with me. However, after Libby died, there were times when I really struggled in worship services. I felt that with all the doubts swirling through my head and a sense of feeling abandoned by God, it would be inauthentic of me to join in the praise, to sing words that I wasn't sure I meant. In one sense, this was true. As I have talked about in 'Braving the elements', moving straight to praising God without first lamenting can be a form of denial. But lament and praise are both forms of worship, and we lose something powerful if we engage in one without the other.

In my case, I had fallen into the trap of believing that because I was struggling with doubt, it would be inauthentic to worship God. At this point one of my wise friends encouraged me that it didn't matter how I felt; what mattered was whether the words were true. If they were, then I could and should sing them.

Added to this, as Eugene Peterson so powerfully articulates:

> In an age of sensation … we think that if we don't feel something there can be no authenticity in doing it. But the wisdom of God says something different: that we can act ourselves into a new way of feeling much quicker than we can feel ourselves into a new way of acting. Worship is an act that develops feelings for God, not a feeling for God that is expressed in an act of worship. When we obey the command to praise God in worship, our deep, essential need to be in relationship with God is nurtured.[127]

When I viewed worship in this way, I found it much easier to engage with it. As a result, I often experienced the turn from the

---

[127] Eugene Peterson, *A Long Obedience in the Same Direction: Discipleship in an Instant Society* (Intervarsity Press, 2019, accessed from Scribd (www.scribd.com)), p55.

darkness of despair to the light of hope. I experienced God's presence and love again, and my perspective shifted from my problems to the power and glory of God.

Doxology as defiance

My wonderful friend Catherine Delve recently wrote a blog post on the importance of praise in the midst of crisis. In this post, she talks powerfully about how praise is an act of defiance in the face of death and suffering.[128] This is precisely how I have always described what worship was like for me after Libby died. Praising God was an act of defiance against the enemy.

In his famous passage about the armour of God, the apostle Paul makes it clear that, as followers of Jesus, our battle is never against flesh and blood. It is 'against the rulers, against the authorities, against the cosmic powers of this present darkness, against the spiritual forces of evil' (Ephesians 6:12). Theologian William Stringfellow made it clear that the principalities and powers of this world are aligned either with the power of death or with the power of life.[129] When we praise God in the middle of our winter seasons, we are aligning ourselves with the power of life, the source of which is God. When we praise God in the middle of our heartache, when winter is at its darkest, we are declaring that, just as death had no power over Jesus, it has no power over us either. It does not and will not have the final word.

---

[128] Catherine Delve, 'Praise as Defiance in the Face of Suffering and Death', WTC Theology, 11th May 2020,
https://wtctheology.org.uk/theomisc/praise-as-defiance-in-the-face-of-suffering-and-death/ (accessed 19th November 2020).
[129] William Stringfellow quoted in Catherine Delve, 'Praise as Defiance in the Face of Suffering and Death'.

Lighting up the darkness

When thinking about the importance of praise in our winter seasons, it's easy to focus on its power to bring change in us, that sense of readjusting our perspective from looking at our situation in despair to focusing on God and so sensing hope rise again. However, praise doesn't just affect us. As Dallas Willard articulates, 'the effect [of worship] is a radical disruption of the powers of evil in us and around us'.[130]

As humans made in His image, God calls us to rule and reign with Him and to work to extend His Kingdom. When we worship God, we are operating in this true God-given calling. Just as when God created the world He spoke into the darkness and brought light and life, the words of our worship speak into the darkness of our situations to call out the light of life. Our words have power and become the catalyst for the inbreaking of the Kingdom.

As an aside, we must speak out the words of our praise. The Genesis 1 account tells us, 'God said …' It wasn't the thoughts of God that created life; it was His spoken words. It's the same for us: there is power in speaking God's life-giving words out loud.

I love the story in 2 Chronicles 20, which speaks of the power of worship when it comes to fighting battles. In the biblical account, we read that the people of Judah were facing the vast combined force of the Moabites, Ammonites and Meunites. I have always found it intriguing that King Jehoshaphat essentially decided to put the worship band at the front of the army. It turns out that this was a master stroke from Jehoshaphat because it was as the worship started that 'the LORD set an ambush against the Ammonites, Moab, and Mount Seir, who had come against Judah' (2 Chronicles 20:22). The prophetic word that the people of Judah had received was

---

[130] Dallas Willard, *Renewing the Christian Mind: Essays, Interviews and Talks* (HarperOne, New York, 2016), p43.

fulfilled; they did not have to fight the battle. Their role was to take up their positions; stand firm and see the deliverance that God would give them (2 Chronicles 20:17).

This is our role in the middle of winter. Ultimately, the battle isn't ours; it's God's. Our call is to take up our positions and stand firm. There are some days when simply standing will feel like the most enormous of tasks. But when we do this, when we stand firm and praise Him in the midst of the pain and confusion, when we speak words of life over the death we see all around us, we will see the disruption of the powers of this world. We will see the darkness pushed back by light. We will see the enemy retreat and the Kingdom of God advance. We will bear witness to the truth that 'the light shines in the darkness, and the darkness did not overcome it' (John 1:5).

Walk it out

- You might like to collect your own Bible verses that you find particularly encouraging and either commit them to memory or write them on sticky notes and put them around your home.

- I would encourage you to find a way of engaging in sung worship. It might be that this is in your own home, in the car, in a church – wherever works for you.

- Spend some time meditating on the opening words of John's Gospel: John 1:1-14.

Comfort food

One does not live by bread alone, but by every word that

comes from the mouth of the LORD.

Deuteronomy 8:3

The power of story

One of Charlie's daily routines is his bedtime story. I love this time of day with him as we snuggle up in bed together. We both particularly love the stories written by Julia Donaldson, like *The Gruffalo*, *The Highway Rat* and *Stick Man*. Charlie loves them because they are funny, and the artwork is always beautiful. I love them because each one teaches a different lesson about how to live life well.

Stories have tremendous power to form us – either to deform us or to transform us. They move our hearts either towards or away from God. Stories have far more power to move us into action than mere facts do. For example, think about the difference between hearing the statistics about the number of people who have died from coronavirus and hearing the personal story of someone you know whose loved one died as a result of contracting the virus. Which is more likely to move you to action?

Curating media

In his book *The Common Rule*, one of the habits that Justin Whitmel Earley has established is what he calls 'curating media'. I love the use of the word 'curate' here. It conjures up the beauty of an exhibition at a museum or gallery, where the curator has intentionally chosen which pieces to use, and where, generally, less is more. What's more, it speaks of creating something beautiful.

Curating media works in just the same way. It is about being intentional about what we allow to enter our thought life in the form of what we engage with through television, social media, YouTube and films. Justin has set a limit of four hours a week on his media. He also runs everything he engages with through the filter of beauty, community and justice.[131] Essentially, he's asking the question, does this speak to me about beauty or the importance of community, or is it an issue of justice which, as a follower of Jesus, I need to engage with?

One of the things I did when Libby died was to stop watching the news. It's a strategy that I employed during the coronavirus crisis too, where I limited myself to checking the news once a day. It was a self-protection thing – when life is tough, I don't need to hear more bad news.

Sometimes I think we worry that if we don't watch the news and are not informed about current affairs we are somehow shutting off from the world. We can worry that we are ignoring the problems of the world, hence impacting our formation as people and our engagement with the world as Christians.

Interestingly, though, Shawn Achor says, 'Psychologists have found that people who watch less TV are actually *more* accurate judges of life's risks and rewards than those who subject themselves to the tales of crime, tragedy and death that appear

---

[131] Justin Whitmel Earley, *The Common Rule*, pp111-127.

night after night on the ten o'clock news.'[132] This might seem counter-intuitive until we realise that watching more news, which is often sensationalised and one-sided, changes a person's view of reality.[133] As a result, these people tend to catastrophise and see the worst in a situation. Personally, I know that the more time I spend watching or reading the news, the more a sense of hopelessness can set in as I reflect on the scale of some of the global problems. When we were walking through our winter season, not engaging with lots of news was my way of not focusing on yet more darkness but instead turning to find the light. On a more practical level, we'll find that we have a lot more time for some of the other practices that follow if we curate our news intake.

I want to be clear here. I'm not advocating that we don't engage with any news at all; I'm simply saying that we need to be discerning about how much news we take in and how often we do so. We also need to be careful about the source of our news; looking to journalism that consults experts, rather than social media, for example.

Although I didn't know it at the time, after we lost Libby, I basically utilised Justin's 'beauty, community and justice' filter, and it is something I continue to do. I can tell you there's an awful lot of stuff that doesn't make it through this filter. I watch a lot less television and am far more intentional about what I read. Having experienced the death of a child, my heart is a lot more tender than it used to be. I feel the pain of others at a much more visceral level.

One of the other big things that does not make it through my filter very often is Facebook (or any form of social media, for that matter). I know that, for many, this is a fantastic platform for staying in touch with people around the world. However, I was increasingly finding that I would feel worse, not

---

[132] Shawn Achor, *The Happiness Advantage: The Seven Principles that Fuel Success and Performance* (Virgin Books, London, 2011), p53.
[133] Shawn Achor, *The Happiness Advantage*, p53.

better, after any time on social media. As I mentioned in a previous chapter, I have a great temptation to compare myself to others, so engaging with these platforms is not helpful for me. I am far better off actually going and meeting a friend for coffee or dropping them a message rather than using Facebook to connect with them.

Chewing on God's word

Just as our dietary choices are important when it comes to our bodies being healthy, we need to make good choices about what we feed our souls. Having made the decision not to fill our minds with 'junk food', we fill them with the words of God; this is comfort food at its very best. We need to dwell in the story of God and the truth of His word.

All of that said, when Libby died, I found it hard to engage with the Bible. During this time, one of the most helpful contemplative practices that I discovered was the practice of *Lectio Divina*, or Divine Reading. In his book *Finding Sanctuary*,[134] Benedictine Abbot Christopher Jamison makes the point that, in our society, reading generally is entirely functional. It is all about gathering more information that will aid us in our quest to understand and control life. But this is not how it always was. Before the foundation of universities in the thirteenth century, reading was about growing in wisdom. It didn't matter whether the text was sacred or secular. Jamison says, 'In this world view, God wants to remedy our disordered lives and the ultimate God-given remedy is to learn wisdom ... to read a text of arts or sciences is to be engaged in the work of your salvation, not acquiring information.'[135] In contrast to informational knowledge, wisdom is deeply practical. Growing in wisdom helps us to live a more integrated and balanced life; a more fully

---

[134] Abbot Christopher Jamison, *Finding Sanctuary: Monastic Steps for Everyday Life* (Orion Books Ltd, London, 2006).
[135] Abbot Christopher Jamison, *Finding Sanctuary*, p62.

human life. Wisdom has the power not just to inform our lives but also to transform them.

As well as becoming all about information gathering, reading has become fast. We live in an age of 'more' and 'faster'. When it comes to reading, it's all about how much information we can assimilate as quickly as possible. People take classes in speed reading and boast about how quickly they can read a book or an article. It's like fast food – purely functional – but, like good food, we are meant to savour and enjoy a beautifully written book, not rush through it. To extend the metaphor, by always going after more and faster, we end up with indigestion! We don't ever really process what we have read and therefore don't extract the real value of it.

On this point, how often do you go back and read the same novel or book? One Christmas, I was gifted a book subscription. In order for the bookshop to select books I might like, I had to fill in a questionnaire about my reading tastes and habits. One question in particular stumped me. It was this: 'If you had to pick one book off your bookshelves now to read again, that has been a companion to you through your life, which book would it be?' I realised how infrequently I reread books. Then I thought about Charlie and how he loves to watch or read the same things, a habit all children have, but adults often lose. There is power in repetition, though. The more I reread a particular story, the more I come to love and treasure it. And each time I read it, I see different things in the story or details I missed the previous time.

Before discovering *Lectio Divina,* I know I took this attitude towards reading into my engagement with the Bible. I was reading for information; very rarely would I sit with the same passage, reading and rereading it, really savouring it and allowing God to speak to me through it. My Bible reading always felt hurried, too, something I would try to squeeze in at the beginning of the day. I also felt a pressure to have read through the entire Bible. I'd read vast chunks at a time. If I'm honest, in part this was simply to be able to say to myself and others that I had read the whole Bible.

It's not wrong to study the Bible, to dissect it, interrogate it, if you like. In fact, this is key to the process of discovering theological and doctrinal truths. Moreover, it's vital that we do read the whole Bible to get a sense of the grand narrative of God. For me, the issue was that this was generally how I always read the Bible. Too often, I read the Bible to glean more information. As Dietrich Bonhoeffer says, I was reading the Bible thinking about how I would pass it on, rather than approaching it as a love letter written to me by God where, rather than asking what information I need to extract from this, I ask, 'What does this say to me?'[136] To use the analogy of eating, I was stuffing myself with the Bible, rather than taking bite-sized morsels and chewing on them, meditating on them, letting God speak to me through them and as a result do something in me, to change and transform me.

Lectio Divina is a way of approaching the Bible to encounter God and grow in wisdom. In this practice, we come to the Bible believing that it is the living word of God and therefore has the power to transform and change us as we engage with it. As Abbott Jamison says, in *Lectio*, rather than imposing our questions on the text, we allow the text to question us.[137] We let the text come to us. And rather than reading a long passage, in *Lectio Divina* we pick a short passage, maybe a Psalm or a story from one of the Gospels. In this way, we exchange breadth for depth.

Crucially, practising *Lectio Divina* also gets us to slow down as we go through the stages of reading the passage at least twice, reflecting on it, savouring one word or phrase that has caught

---

[136] Dietrich Bonhoeffer, quoted in, 'Prayer Tool: How to do the Lectio Divina', https://downloads.24-7prayer.com/prayer_course/2019/resources/pdfs/21%20How%20to%20do%20the%20Lectio%20Divina.pdf (accessed 20th November 2020).
[137] Abbot Christopher Jamison, *Finding Sanctuary*, p64.

our attention, praying and responding and then resting with God in His word. There is no hurry to *Lectio Divina*.

As a result of engaging with the Bible in this way, people often find that they carry the words of the passage with them into their day – it helps them to meditate on the words of Scripture in their daily lives.[138]

I have had some really precious times of intimacy with God through practising *Lectio Divina*. Through slowing down, coming to a text humbly asking God what He wants to show me through the passage and how He wants to speak to me, reading the text repeatedly and spending time with God in silence afterwards, God has done some deep soul work with me. He has been revealing more of who He is and, in this light, who I am in Him. When we walked through our winter season, practising reading the Bible like this became one of the key ways that I intentionally focused on God and became aware of His presence.

Study God

As I have talked about in an earlier chapter, when Libby died, I was in the middle of a theology course with WTC. One of the first decisions I made after Libby's death was to go back to WTC and complete my course. I have always loved learning and my family joke about the number of degrees I have; I think Jon lives in fear of me announcing that I'm going to embark on yet another course. Joking aside, I think the love of learning is an important part of how God made me. It has and continues to be one of the primary ways in which I engage with God and sense His presence.

For this reason, being within the WTC community as we walked through our winter season was absolutely the right place for me to be. It gave me a safe place to unpack some of the big

---

[138] For a brilliant and practical introduction to *Lectio Divina*, see 'Prayer Tool: How to do the Lectio Divina'.

213

questions that I was asking. More than this, I was surrounded by wise people, in both the lecturers who taught me and my fellow students. These people helped me as I wrestled with working out my theology (how I thought about God) in the middle of my winter season.

As I have unpacked in a previous chapter, reflecting on my theology, my ways of thinking about God, was an important part of how I was able to walk through winter with God by my side. How I thought about God affected how I experienced Him in the midst of the pain and loss. In addition to this, studying God was a way for me to be intentional about filling my mind with things that are true, pure, excellent and praiseworthy (see Philippians 4:8).

You might not fancy the idea of an academic theology course, but in our modern world there are so many ways to study God, from the teaching in our local church to podcasts, blogs or books. There are also lots of different Christian conferences that offer some fantastic opportunities to hear excellent teaching. In our winter season, in my quest to feed my soul I employed all of the above.

Walk it out

- Have a look back at your habit log and work out how much time you spend engaging with media. Then spend some time prayerfully considering what curating your media might look like. What would be a good weekly time limit for you?

- Having decided on a limit for your media, you might like to try what John Mark Comer calls a 'habit swap'.[139] Here you replace some of the time you would have spent on media with a different practice – for example, taking some time for silence and solitude, engaging in *Lectio Divina,* listening to a teaching podcast or reading a book you have been meaning to read, or meeting with a friend. Or maybe sign up for a Bible study course.

- You might like to practise *Lectio Divina* using Psalm 1:1-3.

---

[139] John Mark Comer, 'Discovering your Identity and Calling: Part 6 Habit Swap', https://practicingtheway.org/identity/part-six (accessed 3rd December 2020).

Warmth

Then the Lord God said, 'It is not good that the man should be alone; I will make him a helper as his partner.'

Genesis 2:18

I have always loved watching David Attenborough documentaries. The sheer beauty, variety and complexity of the natural world never ceases to amaze me. When thinking about writing this chapter, I was reminded of one of these documentaries which follows a colony of emperor penguins as they attempt to survive an Antarctic winter.[140] To survive the extreme conditions of winter in the Antarctic, these penguins have to work together. The most iconic way they do this is to huddle together to share body warmth. Astonishingly, it's in the inhospitable conditions of an Antarctic winter that emperor penguin chicks are born and nurtured.

I often think of the emperor penguins when reflecting on the importance of being in loving, supportive relationships when we walk through winter. These relationships bring us in from the cold of isolation and loneliness. Just like the penguins, if we huddle together with others, we will not only keep warm through the harshest winter, but we can also birth new life in these inhospitable conditions.

---

[140] BBC, *Dynasties: The Greatest of their Kind*, Series 1, Episode 2: 'Emperor' BBC 2018.

Made for connection

When talking about loneliness, it's essential to separate it from being alone. A person can be alone and be perfectly content. Equally, you can be surrounded by people and be lonely. Loneliness is the feeling we get when our need for rewarding social contact and relationships is not met. It is the feeling of being 'out in the cold'.

Human beings are wired for connection. Brené Brown articulates, 'As infants, our need for connection is about survival. As we grow older, connection means thriving – emotionally, physically, spiritually and intellectually.'[141]

The need for connection is something that the Bible speaks about from the outset. Genesis 2:1-17 gives us the account of God's creation of Adam and describes how God placed Adam in the Garden of Eden to tend and watch over it. We are then told that God realised it was not good for Adam to be alone. In contrast to the creation account in Genesis 1, where God repeatedly declares the creation 'good' or 'very good', this is the first 'not good' in the Bible. Crucially, it comes *before* the Fall, when the relationship between God and humanity was close, intimate and untainted by sin.

What does God do to correct this 'not good'? He creates Eve to be a helper for Adam in the task of tending the garden. The word used for 'helper' is the Hebrew word *ezer,* and it is the same word that is used in other passages in the Bible when God is described as giving us help (Psalm 20:2; 115:11). While I do not want to get into a debate about the roles of men and women, this is significant, as we can often think of a helper in subordinate terms, that Adam was the leader and Eve was there to support and help. The fact that God is described using the same word should make us stop and think.

It is also important that God created Eve from the side of Adam – from one of his ribs. She was created to walk alongside

---

141 Brené Brown, *I Thought it Was Just Me,* p xxvi.

him and co-labour with him. We are made for relationship, both vertically with God and horizontally with each other. In the same way that we need God, we need each other.

Loneliness kills

In his TED talk entitled 'What Makes a Good Life?',[142] American psychiatrist and Harvard Professor Robert Waldinger unpacks the results from the Grant Study, the longest study on happiness ever conducted. This unique study has followed the same group of 724 men year after year for seventy-five years since 1938. Around sixty of the men are still alive and in their nineties. The men came from two different social groups. The first group started the study when they were at Harvard University. The second group came from Boston's poorest neighbourhoods, from some of the most troubled and disadvantaged families in 1930s Boston.

What have the researchers learned from this incredible study? 'The lessons aren't about wealth or fame or working harder and harder. The clearest message we get … is this: Good relationships keep us happier and healthier. Period.'[143]

The results from this study are backed up by other studies which show that being socially isolated increases a person's risk of premature death by up to 30 per cent, which means that social isolation can be as bad for your health as obesity.[144] Science is now proving that loneliness can actually kill us.

---

[142] Robert Waldinger, 'What makes a good life? Lessons from the Longest Study on Happiness',
https://www.ted.com/talks/robert_waldinger_what_makes_a_good_lif e_lessons_from_the_longest_study_on_happiness/transcript (accessed 20th November 2020).
[143] Robert Waldinger, 'What makes a good life?'
[144] Julianne Holt-Lunstad, Timothy B Smith, Mark Baker, Tyler Harris and David Stephenson, 'Loneliness and Social Isolation as Risk Factors for Mortality: A Meta-Analytic Review', *Perspectives on Psychological Science*, Volume 10, March 2015, pp227-237.

I believe that one of the enemy's primary tactics is isolation. Once he has us on our own, we are more vulnerable to listening to lies about who God is and who we are. For example, when we were walking through our winter season, the times when I was isolated or alone were the times when I was most vulnerable to listening to the lies that said, 'God isn't trustworthy, He doesn't really love you, He can't help you, you'll need to sort this out yourself.' Or the lies would be about my identity that I was worthless because I was struggling to have children, or that the miscarriages and Libby's death were my fault.

Once we start listening to the lies, we are far more likely to change our behaviour. For example, when I allowed myself to doubt God's character or His timing, I was tempted to take matters into my own hands. I would try to control the situation and look to find solutions to the problem I was facing because, clearly, God wasn't doing anything.

Or if I listened to the lies about my identity, it would lead me to a dark place of believing that I was worthless, unlovable and insignificant. Believing that no one would want me around when I was so low, I would withdraw and hide away from friends and family. There were even times when I thought about telling Jon to leave me, because I was the problem; the issue was with my body. If he were to leave me, he could find someone else who would be able to give him the children it seemed I couldn't.

Going into hiding

Why are we tempted to isolate ourselves from others when we are struggling? Going back to Genesis, this time to the story of the Fall in Genesis 3, we see the same dynamics at play that I have described above. The story begins with the serpent asking Eve a question: 'Did God say, "You shall not eat from any tree

https://journals.sagepub.com/doi/abs/10.1177/1745691614568352 (accessed 20th November 2020).

in the garden"?' (Genesis 3:1). The big mistakes that Eve makes are not only to listen but also to engage in a conversation with the serpent. Really, she should have exercised her God-given authority and told the talking snake to, in no uncertain terms, 'Sling it!' But this is not what happens. Instead, a dialogue in which the serpent questions God's character ensues. Eve goes from listening to the serpent to believing his lies, and what is the result? From this place, she takes the fruit from the Tree of the Knowledge of Good and Evil and eats it. She then gives it to Adam, and he eats it too.

Having eaten the fruit, the Bible says that 'the eyes of both were opened, and they knew that they were naked' (Genesis 3:7). For the first time, humanity experiences shame, and this shame fractures their relationship with God and their relationship with each other.

What is shame? As the writer Alan Mann articulates, it is a complex condition, but common to experiences of shame is a theme of self-judgement.[145] While they might look alike, shame is very different from guilt. 'Guilt … is a moral emotion. That is, it tends to be concerned with the other.'[146] It is the sense of having wronged another person or broken the law. Guilt can be relatively easily resolved by asking for forgiveness and repaying the wronged party in some way. Shame, on the other hand, is a much more amorphous emotion. It is the voice in our head that tells us there is something wrong with us. Shame turns us in on ourselves in self-judgement. As a result, shame causes us to hide from other people. It cuts our connection with others because we live in fear of being exposed for who we truly are.[147]

Shame is a universal human emotion; it is something that we all experience. It comes from believing any of the lies of identity articulated in the 'Who am I?' chapter. Believing these lies leads to a feeling of not being or having enough. Not being intelligent

---

[145] Alan Mann, *Atonement for a Sinless Society* (Cascade Books, Eugene, 2015), p25.

[146] Alan Mann, *Atonement for a Sinless Society*, p25.

[147] Alan Mann, *Atonement for a Sinless Society*, p27.

enough, pretty enough, strong enough, capable enough, etc. The list goes on – generally it's a feeling of not being good enough to be loved and accepted. As Francis Weller writes, 'Shame closes the heart to self-compassion. We live with an internal state best characterized as self hatred.'[148] Shame is our internal negative voice, in my case 'Negative Norma', which constantly speaks to us about our worthlessness.

In the same way that Adam and Eve's shame at their nakedness made them sew fig leaves to cover themselves, shame makes us create our own 'fig leaves' to hide the parts of us that we don't want others to see. Not only does shame make Adam and Eve attempt to hide their nakedness, but it also makes them attempt to hide from God. Again, we see this in our own lives too. Sometimes our shame is so great that it's not enough to create a 'fig leaf' to cover it; we feel we have to isolate ourselves from others altogether. We fear having the parts of us that we are ashamed of exposed and opening ourselves to the criticism and judgement of others.

When winter seasons blast through our lives, the last thing we need is to be 'out in the cold' of loneliness and isolation. More than ever, we need to feel connected to others. Like the emperor penguins, we need to 'huddle in' with others. The antidote to shame is to know that we are seen and loved by God and by other people, to know we are accepted for who we truly are. How do we do this? I believe there are two keys to combating shame in our lives. These are the subjects of the following chapters.

---

[148] Francis Weller, *The Wild Edge of Sorrow*, p34.

Walk it out

- Does the idea that shame is a generalised sense of not being enough resonate with you?

- You might like to review your reflections from the 'Who am I?' chapter on the lies you believe when it comes to your identity. Can you see how these lead to shame, and keep you in hiding from God and others?

- Spend some time with the Genesis 3 account of the Fall. Read it through several times and allow God's Holy Spirit to speak to you. What words or phrases resonate for you?

Anam cara

A sweet friendship refreshes the soul.

Proverbs 27:9 (*The Message*)

I often speak at churches about our experiences of baby loss. After one such talk, a young couple came up to me in tears (not unusual given the subject matter) and shared with me that their son had died at around twenty weeks of pregnancy the same year that Libby died. They had a faith, but ever since the death of their son they had not been able to go to church. As we talked further, they shared that, on the advice of medics, they had made the really tough decision to terminate their pregnancy because their son had a life-limiting disability. As Christians, making this decision had led to shame, and it was this shame that made them hide from God and from the community who could best support them and walk with them through this. As a result, they had not been to church since their son died.

What I love about this story is that God is truly the God who sees us.[149] As Psalm 139 reminds us, even our best attempts at hiding from Him are futile. If God were an angry, vengeful God, this would be a scary prospect, but He isn't. Our heavenly

---

[149] When Hagar runs away from Sarah to the wilderness, she has an encounter with God who encourages her to return to Sarah. God promises Hagar that He will multiply her offspring. In response, Hagar names God *El-roi* which means 'God who sees' (Genesis 16:1-16).

Father is a God who is 'merciful and gracious, slow to anger, and abounding in steadfast love and faithfulness' (Exodus 34:6). God had seen this couple; He knew them, and He knew that what they needed most was to be able to stop hiding and to share their experience with others. They needed to experience the healing that comes from being understood and loved. Rather than feeling judged and ostracised, they needed to know they belonged.

How did God do this? Through a faithful friend who had walked with this couple and who gently encouraged them to go back to church. They had listened and picked a local church at random, ending up in the church where I was speaking that day and sharing our experience of walking through a very similar kind of suffering. God knows we need each other.

Ordinary courage

So how do we counter shame? Francis Weller suggests that there are three steps. The first is to move from seeing ourselves as worthless to realising that we are wounded. We have a deep wound when it comes to our connection with our true identity as beloved sons and daughters of God. The second step is to move from self-contempt to self-compassion. When I can take a step back from the voice of 'Negative Norma', I realise that I speak to myself in ways that I would never speak to a friend. The compassion we extend to others we need to cultivate for ourselves. The third step is something that Brené Brown argues is the primary weapon against shame, moving from silence to sharing.[150] This step takes courage. Brown calls this 'ordinary courage', which she describes as the ability to 'speak honestly and openly about who we are and about our experiences'.[151] The couple I have just talked about were hugely courageous to share their story with Jon and me. God honoured this courage, and

---

[150] Francis Weller, *The Wild Edge of Sorrow*, pp34-35.
[151] Brené Brown, *I Thought it Was Just Me*, p xxiv.

that day He began the process of healing that they both so desperately needed.

I have often joked that being open with people about my insecurities and failures is a lot like getting physically naked. I guess it is in a way; it is taking away the 'fig leaves' that I have sewn together to cover the parts of me that I don't want others to see. It's important to remember that we don't need to be vulnerable with everyone – much like getting physically naked, really!

Joking apart, though, this is an important point: while we need to make sure that we are not on our own as we journey through tough times, we don't need to be open and vulnerable with everyone we meet.

Intriguingly, when Danes were asked what the ideal number of people for *hygge* was, the answer was three or four.[152] What's more, the Harvard happiness study showed that it wasn't the quantity of relationships that was important, but the quality of these relationships.[153] We see this in the Gospel accounts of Jesus' relationships. While Jesus chose twelve disciples, at key moments in His ministry, such as the raising of Jarius' daughter and His transfiguration, He took just Peter, James and John with Him (Mark 5:35-43; 9:2-8).

To experience the warmth of love and acceptance that friendship offers, we need to cultivate deep relationships built on trust, relationships where we know what we say is not going to be shared with the whole world. It's within these relationships that we can, as it were, come in from the cold of loneliness and isolation through being vulnerable.

Anam cara

Early Christians in Ireland had a tradition of regularly meeting with an *anam cara*, a 'soul friend'. They valued this relationship

---

[152] Meik Wiking, *The Little Book of Hygge*, p62.
[153] Robert Waldinger, 'What makes a good life?'

so highly that they taught that 'a person without a soul friend was like a human body without a head'.[154]

Our soul is our true self; it is the God-given animating life force in all of us. However, as Parker Palmer movingly writes, 'The soul is like a wild animal – tough resilient, savvy … yet exceedingly shy.'[155] Palmer goes on to talk about how the way to see a wild animal is not to go crashing through the woods, but to walk quietly and often to sit in silence for long periods. Only then will you be graced with the sight for which you have come looking.

We all need *anam caras*. People who will help us 'stake out our soul', if you will. People who will help us to walk more quietly and slowly and learn to sit in silence for as long as it takes for the shy creature that is our true self to make an appearance.

I consider myself so blessed with the amazing people that God placed in my life to act as soul friends as I walked through winter. Jon is my closest and dearest soul friend. As I said right at the beginning of this book, Jon is a daily reminder to me of God's grace; he is the most loyal, faithful, gentle, funny and loving husband. He was and continues to be the right man to walk with me through the trauma of baby loss, a journey that we will be on for the rest of our lives. As our vicar said at Libby's thanksgiving service, Jon is my brick – although between you and me I think he would have preferred to have been described as a rock!

While Jon and I had each other as we walked through winter, we also needed our Christian community around us. We both needed others, with different strengths and gifts to whom we could turn. To use the metaphor of the emperor penguins from the previous chapter, while we could help each other stay warm, to be able to do this for the long winter, we needed the love and warmth of a larger community.

---

[154] Ray Simpson, *A Guide for Soul Friends: The Art of the Spiritual Companion* (Kevin Mayhew, Stowmarket, 2008), p6.
[155] Parker Palmer, *Let Your Life Speak*, p7.

Jon and I were so fortunate to be surrounded by the most wonderful community, both within our families and through friendships. All these people helped us withstand the coldest, darkest, most bleak parts of winter. And, like the emperor penguin community, they helped us to birth and nurture new life in the middle of winter. These relationships only sustained us in the way they did because they were built on an ability to be vulnerable and authentic about what was really going on and how we felt.

I vividly remember one of my soul friends ringing me the day after Libby had died and saying to me, 'I'm here, I'm going to walk this with you for as long as it takes.' She didn't know at this point that it would be years, but she faithfully and prayerfully walked alongside me the whole time. She was someone I trusted deeply and, as a result, she was one of the first people I called when I had more miscarriages after Libby, and she was also one of the first friends I told when I was pregnant with Charlie. She never once tried to hurry me through winter, nor was she shocked by anything I shared with her. She simply listened and helped me to process all that happened. Her commitment to us was costly to her, but I can't put into words how much it meant to Jon and me to know that she was there walking with us.

Spiritual accompaniment

I am fully aware that I have been a little loose in my use of the term *anam cara*. Strictly speaking, a true soul friend relationship is different from a normal friendship. It is more like the relationship between a mentor and the one being mentored.[156] I was blessed in my journey through winter with this type of soul friend in the form of my spiritual director.

As a result of my winter pilgrimage, one of my favourite verses in the Bible is, 'Be still, and know that I am God' (Psalm

---

[156] For more on this see Ray Simpson, *A Guide for Soul Friends*.

46:10). I've always loved this verse, but it developed particular meaning when I realised that the Hebrew word *raphah*, which we translate 'be still', means 'to let drop, to sink, to relax'. My spiritual director has encouraged and challenged me in equal measure to be still and befriend my soul by letting my grip drop, opening my hands and sinking into God's love.

By now, you have probably realised that this sense of letting go, of surrendering to God's love, is a recurring theme in this book. I can't overstate the importance of this when it comes to growing in awareness of our true God-given identity. This message has become so key to my own relationship with God that I start each day in silence, just sitting for five or maybe ten minutes with my hands open on my lap to symbolise my intent to let go of all I am carrying and sink into God's love for me.

Guard your heart

Executive coach and author Charles Feltman describes trust as 'choosing to risk making something you value vulnerable to another person's actions'.[157] When we are in the middle of a season of loss, our hearts are exceptionally tender. Often the things we share are of great value. For example, during our season of loss, what I wanted to talk about was my experience of Libby's death and the other babies I miscarried. Talking about my experiences was like trusting people with my children. More than this, all that I was walking through, the stripping-back that all the questions had led to, meant that when I talked with trusted people, I was entrusting them with my soul.

I learnt quite quickly who the people were that I could trust and those who, through no fault of their own, were not people with whom I could be vulnerable. I have a card that I doubt I'll ever send, but I bought it because the sentiment resonates with

---

[157] Charles Feltman, quoted in Brené Brown, *Braving the Wilderness: The Quest for True Belonging and the Courage to Stand Alone* (Vermilion, London, 2017), p38.

me. It says, 'Please let me be the first to punch the next person who tells you that everything happens for a reason.' This is one of my pet hate phrases and one that I heard after Libby died. Yes, everything does happen for a reason, but sometimes the reason is far from positive.

In my winter journey, I realised that this kind of statement was often about people trying to find their own answer to the 'why?' question that our suffering had prompted for them. More often than not, I think these kinds of comments come from a place of desperation within people who want to be able to explain to themselves why terrible things happen. For Christians, it is also often about trying to shore up their faith and understanding of God's sovereignty.

Tragedies challenge our sense of control, so, at some level, all explanations of why these things happen are about people trying to regain some sense of control. It could be about helping them feel that they are still in control of their lives because the explanation of why you are struggling is something that could never happen to them. Or it might be about trying to convince themselves that God is in control.

The people I trusted enough to be open and vulnerable with were those who never attempted to explain away my pain, to judge me, or in any way to try to tell me what I needed to do to 'fix' the problem. Instead, just like our loving heavenly Father does, they understood that their presence and love was far more important to me than anything else.

Having said all this, I want to add one caveat – no one is perfect. Even those I trust the most in my life say unhelpful things sometimes. One of the other important lessons I learnt was not to expect too much of other people. I have never found a less harsh way of phrasing this, but essentially what I mean is that other people are not God; they are not perfect, and they don't know you as well as He does. The only person who truly knows, accepts and loves you for who you are is God. Other people may come close, but at the end of the day, our first point of reference should be God.

When close friends said unhelpful things, I had a choice to make. I could hold on to the hurt, which meant I risked losing the connection with them. Alternatively, I could choose to extend grace towards them and remember that there are plenty of times where the 'shoe has been on the other foot', so to speak, where I have been unknowingly insensitive or hurtful.

What do I say?

As I finish this chapter, I want to say a brief word about supporting friends and family who are going through winter seasons. How can we be soul friends to them? When I speak about our experiences, I am often approached afterwards by people wanting to know how best to support friends or loved ones going through the pain of loss. If this is you, the best piece of advice I can offer is to turn up and shut up.

In all seriousness, though, I have learnt that the best words for times of deep sadness and suffering are, 'I'm so sorry this is happening to you, and I want you to know you're not alone; I'm here.' That's it. But, crucially, like my friend, you have to follow through on your promise to be there, which is costly. You don't know, when you make that promise, how long you will have to walk through winter with your friend. Take the case of my mum and another friend of ours, who committed to fasting and praying for us every Thursday. They didn't know when they made that commitment that it would be years before they got to enjoy a hearty meal on a Thursday.

The only other piece of advice I have if you are supporting someone walking through suffering is 'comfort in, dump out'. This phrase comes from an article in the *Los Angeles Times* by Susan Silk and Barry Goldman.[158] The article was based on Silk's own experience with breast cancer.

---

[158]Susan Silk and Barry Goldman, 'How not to say the wrong thing', *Los Angeles Times*, 7 April 2013, https://www.latimes.com/nation/la-oe-

Imagine a series of concentric circles. The person(s) to whom the tragedy has happened is in the innermost circle. In our case, this would have been Jon and me. The next circle is immediate family, then close friends, and so on – you get the picture. The advice is simple. We only ever give comfort to those in the rings closer to the centre than we are.

Silk and Goldman make the point, as I have above, that, in general, for those closer to the trauma than us, the best thing we can do is listen. However, if we are going to say anything, don't give advice; just give comfort. We definitely don't tell this person how hard we are finding their situation, or how badly we have been affected by it. I know when we were in the midst of the darkness after Libby died, I barely had the capacity to deal with my own grief, let alone the suffering of others. Other people sharing how hard they were finding it either made me angry, as they clearly had no idea just how bad it was for Jon and me, or I felt guilty for putting them through all of this with us. For this reason, when we find ourselves supporting someone walking through a winter season, it is essential that we have people less closely involved in the situation (further out of the centre) who can support us, people we can 'dump on'. We need to find our own soul friends to walk with us.

0407-silk-ring-theory-20130407-story.html (accessed 20th November 2020).

Walk it out

- Spend some time looking back on your life. Who are the soul friends that God has placed in your life at different times? Spend some time thanking God for these people.

- Who are your soul friends now? What can you do to deepen these relationships? What would courage look like in these relationships?

- If you don't have a mentor or spiritual director, you might like to ask God to place someone in your life who could walk with you in this way.

Sharing the load

For as in one body we have many members, and not all the members have the same function, so we, who are many, are one body in Christ ... We have gifts that differ according to the grace given to us.

Romans 12:4-6

It was no surprise to me that Charlie Mackesy's book, *The Boy the Mole, the Fox and the Horse*, fast became a bestseller. Each page is filled with beauty and wisdom, and a good dose of humour too. One of my favourite pictures has the little boy asking the horse what the bravest thing he's ever said is. The horse's response is, 'Help.'[159] This articulates perfectly the second weapon we have in our fight against shame: the ability to ask for help.

As well as keeping us in hiding, making us afraid to show people who we really are because we fear that we are in some way not enough, shame keeps us from asking others for help. Many of us have believed the lie of self-sufficiency, that we should be able to cope. We think that strong people don't ask for help; they just 'suck it up and get on with it'. Needing or asking for help can make us feel very vulnerable. We worry that

---

[159] Charlie Mackesy, *The Boy, the Mole, the Fox and the Horse* (Penguin, Random House, London, 2019).

others will see it as a sign of weakness, an admission that we can't manage on our own, which in our society is not the way we do it. It is much easier to be the one who helps rather than the one in need.

The truth is that, rather than being a sign of weakness, the ability to ask for help is a deeply courageous act of vulnerability. Not only are we allowing others to see what is really going on, but we are also placing ourselves in another's hands, meaning we are no longer in control. What if they don't do things the way we would? What if they take risks we wouldn't? What if they don't do it as well as we could? If we are used to being the responsible one, the one who does things well and has life 'together', asking others for help and releasing control to them is a hugely courageous thing to do.

I don't want to be a burden

Alternatively, rather than worrying about being seen as weak if we ask for help, one of the other reasons we might isolate ourselves from others when we are in a winter season is because we want to protect them from our pain. I have heard this so often; people don't tell family or friends that they are suffering or going through a difficult time because they don't want to be a burden to them. Life is complex, everyone has their own cares and concerns, and we worry that we will just be adding to that burden.

Or perhaps we are worried about becoming the 'needy' one. We all know people who have decided for one reason or another not to take responsibility for their own lives. These are people who live on the opposite side of the fence I have just described. Rather than not wanting to ask for help, they are always asking for help, seemingly unable to manage everyday things without the help of others.

The apostle Paul addresses this in Galatians 6:2-5, where we seem to have a contradiction at play. Paul tells the Galatian Christians that they should 'Bear one another's burdens, and in this way you will fulfil the law of Christ.' Then, only a couple of sentences later, he says, 'For all must carry their own loads.' What does Paul mean?

The key here is to recognise that Paul has purposely used two different words for 'burden' and 'load'. The Greek word used for 'burden' is *baros* and was frequently used to describe a burden too heavy for one person to carry alone. In contrast, the Greek word for 'load', *phortion*, described a backpack-sized load, something that a person would be able to carry on his or her own.[160] The point Paul is making seems more apparent in the New Living Translation of verse 5: 'For we are each responsible for our own conduct.' That is, there are normal responsibilities that come with life for which we are accountable. For example, in our everyday lives we are ultimately responsible for making sure we get enough sleep, eat properly, exercise regularly and manage our finances – I think you get the point.

In contrast, verse 2 is saying that there are times in life when people are overwhelmed, and they need help if they are not to be crushed by the circumstances of their lives. The crisis could be as a result of an unhelpful pattern of behaviour, or it could be a traumatic loss, such as Jon and I experienced. We can't cope with such events on our own; we need the support of others.

Being the wounded Jew

Dame Cicely Saunders was a nurse, researcher and one of the key figures in the founding of the hospice movement in the UK. In her book, *Beyond All Pain*, she says this: 'It is hard to be the wounded Jew, when, by nature, you would rather be the good Samaritan.'[161] However, as she goes on to say, 'the wounded

---

[160] Henry Cloud and John Townsend, *Boundaries: When to Say Yes, How to Say No to Take Control of Your Life* (Zondervan, MI, 2017), p31.
[161] Quoted in Angela Ashwin, *From Pain to Prayer: Opening up to God When Life Is Hard* (Fount Paperbacks, London, 1997), p128.

man and the Samaritan are inseparable. It was the helplessness of the one that brought out the best in the other and linked them together.'[162] I love this. As long as we stay isolated and don't ask others for help, we don't give people the opportunity to help us with the things that they are good at. We don't release them into their gifting.

One of the apostle Paul's favourite metaphors when talking about the Church is the human body. In 1 Corinthians 12 and Romans 12, Paul makes the point that a body is made up of lots of different parts that all have their own job to do. Without each part doing its specific job, the body doesn't function well. Paul says a church community is like the body in that we all have different gifts. Paul's list of gifts is long and includes the gifts of prophecy, faith, encouragement, service, teaching and healing.

Rather than isolating ourselves and trying to cope on our own, what we need to do when winter seasons come is to look to release our friends into their giftings by asking for their help. I know many wonderful people who have the gift of helping others in really practical ways. For example, some people are absolutely brilliant with babies and children and, rather than it being a burden, it is a delight and a privilege to them to look after our child for a couple of hours. Others have a culinary gift. I'm even told that there are people who love cleaning – these people are welcome at my house any time! Other people are great at administration and paperwork.

To put courage in

I don't know about you, but I used to be tempted to think of the gift of encouragement in a somewhat wishy-washy way. I wrongly thought that being an encourager was about saying 'nice' things to people that might help them feel better about themselves. However, this is not what the gift of encouragement is all about. The word 'encouragement' comes

---

[162] Angela Ashwin, *From Pain to Prayer*, p129.

from old French words *en*, meaning 'make, put in' and *corage*, 'courage, heart'.[163] To encourage someone means to put courage in him or her, to give them the heart to keep going. Seen this way, it is much more powerful. We need to seek out these people, the ones who, after spending time with them, we feel like our courage tanks have been 'topped up'. These people will empower us to keep walking through our seasons of pain.

Find your Aaron and Hur

When we were in the midst of our losses, I really struggled with permitting myself to ask a small group of people to pray for me. It felt a little attention-seeking or self-indulgent. Then God reminded me of the account of Israel's battle with the Amalekites in Exodus 17:8-13. In this story, we are told that Moses, Aaron and Hur were at the top of a mountain watching Joshua and the Israelite army. 'Whenever Moses held up his hands, Israel prevailed' (Exodus 17:11). As you would expect, Moses' arms soon became tired. What did Aaron and Hur do? The writer tells us:

> They took a stone and put it under [Moses], and he sat on it. Aaron and Hur held up his hands, one on one side, and the other on the other side; so his hands were steady until the sun set. And Joshua defeated Amalek and his people with the sword.
> *Exodus 17:12-13*

As I reread this story, I felt God say to me, 'You need your own Aaron and Hur, people who will hold you up in prayer when you feel too weary.' So I created a small email group of close friends whom I knew had the gift of intercession and would be

---

[163] 'Encourage', Online Etymology Dictionary, https://www.etymonline.com/word/encourage (accessed 23rd November 2020).

237

able to support me in prayer. Again, rather than seeing this as a burden, those I asked told me that they viewed it as a privilege to be able to help me in this way.

Faith-filled friends

Or what about the gift of faith? When we were in the middle of winter and desperate to see God break in to change the season for us, I became very good at beating myself up about whether I had enough faith for God to act. I would read the Gospel accounts of healing and hear Jesus' words, 'Your faith has healed you,' not as encouragement but as condemnation, believing that I wasn't receiving healing or breakthrough because I didn't have enough faith.

One of the devil's tactics in the spiritual battle is to use Scripture against us – he did it with Jesus, so it's no surprise that he does it with us. These words of Jesus about the importance of faith to those He healed were among the devil's weapons against me – particularly on the days when I didn't feel like I had any faith left, when the sense of spiritual isolation and confusion was too great. I used to describe it as a fog that would come down, and I could no longer see or sense God's presence.

There were other times when I didn't want to put my faith in Jesus to heal our situation because that would lead to hope, and hope was a dangerous thing. Each time I had been pregnant I had hoped that this time would be different, that it wouldn't end in loss, and each time I had seen the hope crushed as we lost one baby after another. Not only did I have to deal with a loss of hope each time, but I had to face grief and spiritual confusion. It felt easier not to raise my expectations faith-wise as it protected me from yet more sorrow.

Then quietly one day, I felt the Spirit whisper a different word to me: 'But what about the times when it wasn't the faith of the person who needed healing that was important? What about all those times when I healed in response to the faith of others?' As I thought I about this, I found myself remembering other Gospel accounts, like the story of the Centurion who comes to Jesus to ask for healing for his servant (Matthew 8:5-13; Luke 7:1-9). Or Jairus, who asks Jesus to heal his daughter (Mark 5:21-43; Matthew 9:18-26). There are several other accounts like these. In all of them, faith is important, but, crucially, Jesus responds to the faith of those interceding for the ones who needed healing. We don't know anything about the faith of Jairus' daughter or the Centurion's servant.

When I felt as though I had no faith left, these stories gave me permission to rely on the truth that God had placed people around us whom He had gifted with the faith to go to Him and intercede on our behalf when I couldn't.

Jesus' hands and feet

Often when I'm talking with Charlie about how Jesus is always with us, he very sensibly says to me, 'But Mummy, I wish I could see Jesus.' I'm with him on this one. There are many times in life when I would love a hug from Jesus, or just to have Him physically present with me. The truth is, however, that Jesus is physically with us in the form of other people He places in our lives to walk with us through winter seasons.

If we have the courage to be vulnerable with others, to let them see the 'real' us and to ask for their help, we will witness the truth of these words outworked in our lives. The love and acceptance we will experience are a reflection of the way our heavenly Father loves and accepts us. Experiencing this love and acceptance is what will keep us warm through the coldest of winters.

Walk it out

- How do you feel about asking others for help? Do you see asking for help as a sign of weakness? How does it feel to let go of control? Are you worried about burdening others?

- Where in your life right now do you need help? Write down anything that comes to mind, no matter how big or small. Then ask God to show you the people in your life who could help you.

- Spend some time reflecting on the account of the raising of Jairus' daughter in Matthew 9:18-26. Imagine yourself in the scene. Who are you? What does Jesus say to you? Journal anything you feel God say to you through this.

Recreation

He makes me lie down in green pastures;

he leads me beside still waters;

he restores my soul.

Psalm 23:2-3

One of the things Sheridan Voysey articulates beautifully in his journey through childlessness is the sense of finding 'your tribe'.[164] Once you start sharing your story of broken dreams and loss, you realise that there is a whole tribe of people out there also trying to come to terms with the loss of dreams. The sense of 'finding my tribe' was something I experienced too. Once I started talking to people, I realised that many others were walking a similar path. It is heartbreaking to me that there are so many members of my tribe, too many people having to walk the path of child loss. At the same time, it has also been a source of encouragement. We have been able to support each other and so keep each other warm in the chill of the isolation and loneliness of our winter seasons.

One winter's day, I was out for a walk with one of my 'tribe'. We had decided to walk from the village that I lived in at the

[164] Sheridan Voysey, 'Your Pain Can Get You Inside This Secret Tribe', https://sheridanvoysey.com/046-your-pain-can-get-you-inside-this-secret-tribe/ (accessed 4th December 2020).

time to a neighbouring village which had an excellent pub where we could toast ourselves by the fire and enjoy a good lunch before venturing home. As it was winter, the footpath that we were walking on was wet and really, really muddy. As a result, walking was hard work – at times we were literally wading through mud – and it was freezing. As we walked, we both reflected on the fact that this is how it feels to walk through grief. It's like struggling through thick mud; each step is difficult, and we have to concentrate hard so that we don't end up on our bottoms in the mud!

Walking through winter seasons of loss is exhausting at a deep soul level. We can feel drained on emotional, physical and spiritual levels. It was during our season of loss that the promise of God in Psalm 23 to restore my soul took on particular significance, as this was what I needed.

What is my soul?

Church culture has tended to be dualistic when it comes to thinking about the soul – seeing it as something separate from the rest of us. Thinking this way has led some to go so far as to think of the soul as the spiritual and 'good' part of us that will last for eternity, while our physical bodies are at best irrelevant, and at worst something from which we need to escape. But this is not the biblical understanding of what our souls are.

The Hebrew word translated 'soul', for example in Genesis 2:7 during the account of the creation of Adam, is *nephesh*. Retreat leader and author Brian Draper writes that this word has 'at least eight derivations: a living being, life, self, a person, desire, passion, appetite and emotion. And it's this breadth of meaning that leads people … to describe *nephesh* as "your whole being".' Brian goes on to explain that what Genesis 2 is saying is 'not that God made a body and popped a soul inside it; instead God brought the dust to life, and the dust became the being, a whole creature in itself'.[165] The biblical understanding of soul is holistic: we are fully integrated creatures, mind, body and spirit. As a result, what happens in one part of our being affects the rest of us. And this is why grief is so draining; the emotions associated with grief manifest themselves in mental, physical and spiritual exhaustion. It follows, then, that when Jesus offers us rest for our souls (Matthew 11:29), this rest will be holistic; it will involve the whole of our being: mind, body and spirit.

Rest for the body

In her book, *An Invitation to Silence and Solitude*, spiritual formation expert Ruth Haley Barton articulates the truth that rest for our souls, learning to rest in God, starts with resting our physical bodies.[166] It begins with meeting the body's basic needs for sleep and nutrition.

Ruth uses the story of Elijah in 1 Kings 19:1-18 to unpack this truth. In this biblical story, Elijah has just had his powerful encounter with the prophets of Baal. Immediately after this, he is threatened with death by Queen Jezebel. Exhausted, Elijah flees into the desert, sits down under a bush and prays that he might die. Then he promptly falls asleep. What does God do? He sends an angel to feed Elijah. Elijah eats and drinks and then sleeps some more. It's only once he has rested physically that Elijah sets off for Mount Horeb, where he meets with God.

In our false separation of body and soul, we have often made the mistake of over-spiritualising resting in God. As a result, we have ignored the needs of our bodies. In my case, what this means is that when I do finally manage to enter silence and solitude with God, the first thing I notice is that I am exhausted. In fact, I often fall asleep in my times of silence. I used to beat myself up about this until I heard Pete Greig, founder of the

---

[165] Brian Draper, *Soulfulness*, p69.
[166] Ruth Haley Barton, *An Invitation to Solitude and Silence: Experiencing God's Transforming Presence* (InterVarsity Press, 2010), pp62-69.

24–7 Prayer movement, talk about how when we fall asleep while praying, we are falling asleep in the arms of our loving heavenly Father. I love this image, and it has helped me to permit myself to fall asleep more often with God. Sleep has so many important health benefits, from reducing our risk of heart attack and cancer to improving mental health.[167] Just like some animals hibernate during winter to conserve energy, we need to prioritise sleep when we are walking through seasons of grief and loss.

As well as sleep, our bodies need food and drink. When we are exhausted, the temptation is to reach for 'quick-fix food' – the stuff that is full of sugar and fat – to get us through. What our bodies really need is healthy, nutritious food that will energise and sustain us.

In just the same way that my friend and I needed to stop for lunch to rest physically, to warm up and to refuel with good food so that we would have the energy to go back into the elements of winter, we need to do the same when walking through winter seasons of life. We need to prioritise physical rest in terms of getting enough sleep and eating well so that we will have the energy to go back out and brave the elements again.

Feeling God's pleasure

When thinking about other ways we can restore our souls, I find it helpful to remember that anything that connects me back to God is going to restore me. As we are fully integrated people, this need not simply be through Bible reading, going to church, etc. We can connect with God in so many different ways.

Since I was a teenager, I have loved to run. Growing up, as well as fell walking with my dad, I did a lot of running with him.

---

[167] For more on the importance of sleep see, Matthew Walker, *Why We Sleep: The New Science of Sleep and Dreams* (Penguin Books, London, 2018), particularly 'Part 2: Why Should You Sleep?'

We even entered a few 10K races together. Dad is Kenyan, a nation known for their middle- and long-distance running prowess. So we used to have some fun by making him wear a poster on his back with the Kenyan flag and the tag line, 'Make your day, pass a Kenyan!' You can imagine some of the smiles this raised from fellow runners as they jogged past him.

We have long known the physical health benefits of exercise, but there is now mounting evidence for its mental health benefits too.[168] I can personally attest to this. After Libby died, being able to go out running was one of the key ways that I managed my mental health. It was one of the ways I restored my soul.

Running continues to be something I enjoy doing. For me, it is as much about the mental health benefits as it is about my physical health. Jon's code for, 'You're in a bad mood,' is, 'Do you need to go for a run?!' I prefer to run outside, and I tend not to take headphones or listen to anything as I run. In part, this is about being fully present to my surroundings, but it's also because I have learnt that one of the ways that God speaks most clearly to me is as I run – probably because I am free from so many of the distractions that crowd in at other times.

Often when I'm out running, I am reminded of the Scottish Olympian Eric Liddell's famous comment, 'When I run, I feel [God's] pleasure.' Don't get me wrong – I am not nearly as talented a runner as Liddell; I'm not going to win any medals. But when I run, I sense God's presence in a profound and tangible way, in terms of both how incredible the human body is and how beautiful the created world is.

You might not enjoy running, but what are the things that you love to do? The things that give you pleasure, and where you sense God's presence with you? It might be bike riding, going for a walk, baking, gardening, tinkering with old cars in

---

[168] Aaron Kandola et al, 'Physical Activity and Depression: Towards Understanding the Antidepressant Mechanisms of Physical Activity', *Neuroscience and Biobehavioural Reviews*, 107 (2019), pp525-539.

the shed, painting or drawing, listening to music, reading, meeting friends for coffee – the list is long. In my experience, God meets us and restores us through the things we love doing. As the writer and retreat leader Paula D'Arcy so beautifully puts it, 'God comes to us disguised as our lives.'[169] So think about what you love, what gives you joy, and then go and do it.

Made for rest

Certain circles within our culture are beginning to recognise afresh the importance of rest. However, in many cases, rest is promoted because it leads to increased productivity.[170] Even rest has been put into the service of the idols of productivity and achievement. While it's true that rest does make us more productive, this is a by-product of rest, not the reason for it.

At the beginning of Genesis 2, we are told that, on the seventh day, after God had completed the creation of the 'heavens and the earth', He rested. Rest restores our souls because it helps to restore the image of God in us. We are created in the image of a resting God. What's more, God created humanity to enjoy His rest. In the Genesis 1 account, God creates humanity on day six. Therefore, as theologian A J Swoboda points out, 'Adam and Eve's first full day of existence was a day of rest, not work.'[171] Swoboda goes on to state, 'The biblical story tells us that to rest one day a week is to be truly human, and to not rest is to be inhuman.'[172] Constant work is dehumanising, humans were made to rest. What's more, the rest that God offers is life-giving, as demonstrated by God's blessing of the Sabbath.

---

[169] Paula D'Arcy – quoted in Richard Rohr, *Breathing Under Water*, p15.
[170] For a good example of this see, Alex Soojung-Kim Pang, *Rest: Why You Get More Done When You Work Less* (Penguin Life, London, 2018).
[171] A J Swoboda, *Subversive Sabbath: The Surprising Power of Rest in a Nonstop World* (Brazos Press, Grand Rapids, 2018), p7.
[172] A J Swoboda, *Subversive Sabbath*, p11.

With this understanding in mind, we can see that it's no mistake that Jesus often chose to heal on the Sabbath.[173] Jesus came to show us what it means to be truly human and to restore us to our God-given identity. Therefore, it makes sense that He should heal on the Sabbath.[174] Jesus used the day of rest to restore and heal broken humanity, to bring people back into the *shalom* (wholeness, completeness and peace) and life-giving blessing of God's Kingdom. Jesus' healing was holistic, healing people's broken bodies, minds and relationships.

The word 'recreation' is derived from the Latin word *recreare*, which means 'to refresh, restore, make anew, revive'.[175] It means to re-create. The way we use this word now, to suggest leisure time or fun, was only first recorded around AD 1400. In this context, we can see that Sabbath is the ultimate recreational day. Jesus used and still uses rest as a means of recreation. He uses it to re-create humanity.

In the Gospel accounts, Jesus teaches that in order to enter the Kingdom of God, we need to 'change and become like children' (Matthew 18:3). What do children do a lot of that, as adults, we seem to lose the ability to engage in? Play. Children play, and this is how they learn. Rest and Sabbath are about learning to play with God.

When we see rest in this way, it gives a much more expansive view of what constitutes rest. Basically, it is anything that heals and restores us, that re-creates the image of God in us, whether that's sleeping or exercise, time alone or time with friends, time with God in the quiet or time spent engaging your mind in

---

[173] The Gospels record seven healing miracles that take place on a Sabbath: Mark 1:21-25; Mark 1:29-31; Mark 3:1-6; Luke 13:10-17; Luke 14:1-4; John 5:1-18; John 9:1-16.

[174] I am grateful to the Old Testament scholar Matt Lynch, for these insights.

[175] 'Recreation', Online Etymology Dictionary, https://www.etymonline.com/word/recreation (accessed 24th November 2020).

something you love to do, like writing or painting. Rest is fun; it is your time to play.

Resisting rest

I think many of us know that we need to rest more, but for many of us it can be a real struggle to prioritise rest in our lives. Why is this? When we walked through our winter season, there were several reasons why I resisted resting.

Self-care is selfish

After Libby died, I had some counselling sessions, and as part of these sessions my counsellor encouraged me to make time each week to do something that was just for me, to do something that I loved doing. Essentially, she was encouraging me to rest. I struggled with this because of an overwhelming sense of guilt that if I were to prioritise myself and the things I like doing, that would in some way be really selfish.

I think many of us believe the lie that self-care is selfish. This can be particularly hard for Christians as we feel the pressure to be out there attending to everyone else's needs, serving everyone else, being compassionate to others. However, as the Irish poet and priest John O'Donohue said, if we can't practise self-compassion, then we close ourselves off to the love all around us.[176] Essentially, we will miss God's loving presence. If we miss God's love, then we can't be loving towards others because our tanks are empty.

Will God provide?

I talked in an earlier chapter about trusting God during our winter seasons of loss to provide all that we need, and to provide enough. One of the primary reasons I resisted rest

---

[176] John O'Donohue, quoted in *Celtic Daily Prayer Book Two: Farther Up and Farther In*, p891.

during our winter season was that I didn't entirely trust God to provide the route out of winter. So I kept working really hard to fix the problem.

Perhaps you resonate with this. Maybe you are struggling financially, so you are reading this and thinking, 'I can't possibly rest; I need to work every hour possible to put a roof over my family's head and food on the table.' Or perhaps you are walking through the pain of the death of a loved one, and you are exhausted on every level but don't feel you can take time off. Trusting God enough to risk resting is huge, and I don't want to belittle it. Like everything related to faith, it's a risk, but it's only by stepping out and giving it a go that we realise that God is trustworthy, and He will fulfil his promise to provide, and to provide enough.

The long shadow of grief

When Libby died, Jon often used to talk about how grief was like a shadow. I have always thought this is a really beautiful way of describing how grief manifests itself. Think about it for a moment – just as we can't escape our shadow, grief is always with us. What's more, in the same way that our shadows are longest at the beginning and end of the day, we often feel grief most strongly first thing in the morning and in the evening. Why is this?

I think it's because in the middle of the day we can distract ourselves with the busyness of life, like our work, caring for children, running a home, or other distractions like email and social media and television. But in those first waking moments or in the quiet of evening before we go to bed, that's when grief hits us. So what do we do? We keep ourselves really busy to numb the pain of grief. I have heard too many people say that the way they manage their grief is to keep busy. The problem with this is that it's avoidance. We are back to running hard in an attempt to outrun the darkness. As we have discussed, this strategy will always fail, and rather than helping to restore and renew our energy, it depletes us even further.

I'm not allowed to have fun

A major reason I resisted rest or any sense of having fun was because, when I did allow myself to relax, to laugh and enjoy myself, I then immediately felt guilty. I felt terrible that I was able to laugh in the middle of such raw grief. 'Negative Norma' told me that I shouldn't be enjoying myself because my daughter had just died.

None of this is true; in fact, quite the opposite – maintaining a sense of humour and allowing ourselves to have fun as we walk through winter is vitally important. As psychologist Andrew Bienkowski writes, 'scientific research shows that humour has great healing powers … laughter has been proven to reduce stress and promote physical and mental wellbeing'.[177]

Too busy to rest

Another reason I struggled to rest during our winter season was linked to my broken sense of identity. As a result of believing a combination of the lies of identity that I unpacked in the 'Who am I?' chapter, I had to stay busy. I had to prove my worthiness and value to myself and others.

I also didn't want to stop and rest because, when I did, when the world around me quietened down, Negative Norma really got going. She would tell me all the many and various ways that I was failing, how I was not good enough at anything. The problem with this is, while I might silence the voice of Negative Norma (temporarily), I would also struggle to hear God's voice.

At its heart, I think rest will always be contested because, through rest, God offers us the gift of restoration and healing. When we rest, we step back into our true God-given identities as beloved children of God, created in His image and made to

---

[177] Andrew Bienkowski with Mary Akers, *One Life to Give: A Path to Finding Yourself by Helping Others* (The Experiment, New York, 2010), pp101-102.

enjoy His rest. Receiving the gift of rest is all part of releasing new life even in the midst of winter; it's all about learning to live a more truly human life.

Start small

As I finish this chapter, I want to make one final point, and that is that rest is not a burden; it is a gift. In *The Message* translation of Matthew 11:28-30, Jesus says, 'I won't lay anything heavy or ill-fitting on you. Keep company with me and you'll learn to live freely and lightly.'

Rest is about learning to live more freely. I don't want you to finish this chapter and think, 'Oh goodness, now I have to find a whole twenty-four hours to rest.' While I would encourage you to explore the practice of Sabbath, I would also say, start small. Start with maybe a morning or an afternoon once a week where you prioritise the things that are restful and life-giving for you. In my experience, starting this way and seeing the effects in terms of living more freely and lightly gave me a taste for more. I pray the same will be true for you.

Walk it out

- Why do you struggle to rest? Journal your thoughts and spend some time talking to God about this.

- When I was walking through our season of loss, my mum and I often talked about having a 'toolbox' of things that I knew would restore me on a soul level. The idea was that, as and when I needed to restore my soul, I could take one of them out of my toolbox. You might like to think about creating your own toolbox.

- We need to be intentional about rest; it doesn't just happen. Plan some time in your diary each week, a morning or an afternoon to engage with some of the activities from your toolbox. You might also like to explore the spiritual practice of Sabbath, giving twenty-four hours for rest.

- Spend some time meditating on Psalm 23. This psalm speaks of trusting God, trusting in His provision, presence, goodness and love. It speaks of trusting God in the same way a sheep trusts the shepherd, or you could say as a child trusts their parents. How would trusting in God in this way impact your ability to rest even in the harshest winter?

Hospitality

Blessed be the God and Father of our Lord Jesus Christ, the Father of mercies and the God of all consolation, who consoles us in all our affliction, so that we may be able to console those who are in any affliction with the consolation with which we ourselves are consoled by God.

2 Corinthians 1:3-4

Not long after Libby died, I remember saying to God that if He wasn't going to give me answers to my questions, then what I needed from Him was to tangibly sense His presence in the midst of the cold and dark of winter. One of the ways God did this was through the gift of the prophetic. The apostle Paul, writing to the church in Rome, says that God is a God who 'calls into existence the things that do not exist' (Romans 4:17). I have seen God do this so many times, both in my life and in the lives of others.

Fragile beauty

For me, one of the most powerful experiences of this prophetic calling-out of new life took place on a visit to Winchester Vineyard church one Sunday in the middle of our winter season.

This particular Sunday, the teaching was on the gift of the prophetic. At the end of the service, the lovely Jo Hemming, who leads the church with her husband Nigel, came up to Jon and me saying she had a picture for us. In this picture, she had seen the most beautiful silver sculpture. What made the sculpture so attractive was that it had lots of gaps in it which allowed light to pass through the structure. While these gaps gave beauty to the structure, it also meant it was very fragile. Jo talked about how she sensed that this sculpture symbolised me, the fragility being a result of all that we were walking through. To stabilise this fragile structure, Jo explained, she'd seen it mounted on a really firm base; this base symbolised Jon.

Jo's picture reminded me of a Japanese art form called Kintsugi, where broken pottery is repaired with gold lacquer. The result is a repaired pot which is more beautiful than what you started with. Reflecting on this and Jo's picture gave me the encouragement that God was creating beauty from my brokenness. Crucially, this new life and beauty would come not from my strength but from my fragility and brokenness.

The upside-down message of the Kingdom is that it's in our brokenness, when we are at our weakest and the forces of this world seem at their strongest against us, that God's power can be most evident. As the apostle Paul wrote in his letter to the Corinthians, it's in our weakness that we are strong (2 Corinthians 12:10). Why? Because it's in this place that, rather than relying on our own strength, we recognise our need for God, which then opens us up to His power working through us in the form of the Holy Spirit.

Scars

I have always found it intriguing that Jesus' resurrected body isn't perfect. He still carries the scars of what He went through. Could this be because it was through His wounding, His death, that He released new life for the whole of creation? As Isaiah prophesied, it would be 'by his bruises we are healed' (Isaiah

53:5). Just like Jesus, in God's hands our wounds and brokenness, rather than leading to death, can be a source of new life. As Henri Nouwen so powerfully articulates, 'the wound that causes us to suffer now, will be revealed to us later as the place where God intimated His new creation'.[178] Jesus calls us to follow Him, and this means that in the same way that He used His wounds to bring healing and life for others, He calls us to use our wounds to bring life to others.

I found this truth hugely helpful when it came to sharing our story. One thing I have always fought against is being defined by what we have lost. While this experience is an integral part of my story, it is not the sum total of who I am. I didn't want to be known as 'the woman who lost babies'. However, rather than seeing my scars as a negative thing, I can now see that, in God's hands, they can be used to release new life, in my life and in the lives of others.

The cracks in the sculpture of my life are how the light of God's love gets in. My experience of grief and loss stripped me right back. This was painful, but ultimately healing, as it brought me to a place where I could experience in new and fresh ways the unconditional love of my heavenly Father, the presence of Jesus in the midst of winter, and the power of the Spirit in my life giving me the ability to grow more fully into my God-given identity.

But cracks don't just let light in; crucially, they let light out too.

The cracks in our lives can be the places where the light of God's love shines out most brilliantly to others. The places of our deepest pain, in God's hands, can become our greatest strength. Whether that's the death of a child or loved one, the loss of our health to a chronic life-limiting illness, the loss of our livelihood or a marriage, or the loss of our innocence

---

[178] Henri Nouwen, *The Wounded Healer: In Our Own Woundedness We Can Become a Source of Life for Others* (Darton, Longman and Todd Ltd, London, 1994), p96.

through abuse as a child – whatever our pain and brokenness, God can use it as a source of healing for others.

A welcome for the weary

As we have explored, walking through winter is exhausting, and it is only by experiencing the comfort, warmth and safety of home that we can keep going. Showing others our scars, sharing our pain, is a very vulnerable thing to do. It's like inviting people into our home and allowing them to wander through the whole house, particularly the parts we haven't had time to tidy up. However, as Nouwen teaches, if we can summon the courage to do this, to show others our scars, we perform the ultimate act of hospitality.

We welcome the weary traveller and invite them to come in and lay their burdens down. When we show others our scars, we invite them in from the cold of isolation and loneliness, into the warmth of fellowship. When we share our pain and brokenness with others, it helps them to know they are not alone. And just as home is a safe place, when we share our scars, we permit others to share their hurts and brokenness with us, safe in the knowledge that they will not be judged. More than this, when we share our experience of God's love in the valleys of life, we invite people to come home to their heavenly Father's house, where they are loved, accepted and safe from any storm.

Don't wait until winter is over

I grew up in a stream of the Church that places a high value on testimony. Why do we tell our stories of what God has done in our lives? Testimony is an important means of praising God and thanking Him for the way He has worked in our lives. It also encourages and inspires faith in others. However, my issue with testimony is that, just like our worship can be lopsided, focused solely on praise to the exclusion of lament, far too often our testimonies can be too. The stories we hear from the front of church are of the praise and thanksgiving variety, the 'mountaintop' experiences of breakthrough.

While these stories can and do inspire faith in others, I have also experienced the opposite. I have sat in too many large gatherings listening to 'mountaintop' testimonies of breakthrough, internally questioning God as to why He has not acted similarly in my life. When we were walking through our winter season, I heard plenty of stories of couples who had seen God break through in a miraculous way to give them children they never thought they'd be able to have. Rather than inspiring faith, this often led me to question my faith.

Every amazing story of God's intervention can raise faith, but it also raises questions. What happens when we don't see breakthrough, when babies die or you can never have your own children, when cancer kills your loved ones, when your business goes bankrupt? Or, on a global scale, when a deadly virus sweeps across the world, killing millions and destroying livelihoods, when wars ravage countries, and when millions are trapped in modern-day slavery and the sex industry. Where is God in all these situations? What happens when we don't see breakthrough? Where are the testimonies from the 'darkest valley' (Psalm 23:4)?

Not all discontent is bad; God often calls to us through our dissatisfaction with the way things are. However, rather than becoming bitter and complaining in our dissatisfaction, God can and does give us a vision of how things could be and calls us to be the answer to our own prayers. My dissatisfaction with the lack of testimony from the valley grew in me a vision and passion for sharing my experience of God's love, presence and power in the midst of my pain. I wanted to be able to say to people, 'He's here too.'

Just like lament, testimony in the middle of loss, when the worst things of life have happened, is a powerful act of faith. Not only this, but it also stirs up faith in others who find themselves in the same place. It helps them to know that they are not on their own, that there are others walking through winter too.

If you find yourself in the midst of a winter season, can I encourage you not to wait until you have a pretty ribbon of breakthrough to put on your story before you tell it to others? Share your story of walking through the darkness with God. Speak of His love, faithfulness and goodness in that place. I promise it will build the faith of others and help them to move from the darkness of despair to the light of hope.

Crucially, in Paul's famous passage about God's power being made perfect in our weakness, the context is an unanswered prayer (2 Corinthians 12:7-10). Paul is writing about his 'thorn in the flesh' that, despite Paul asking three times, God did not remove. We don't know what the thorn was for Paul, but what we do know is that God promised Paul, and He promises us, that His grace is sufficient for us. In His hands, our weaknesses are our strength. Having seen the truth of this in my life, I am now happy to echo Paul's words and 'boast all the more gladly of my weaknesses' because I know they are the conduit for the healing power of Jesus' love to flow through my life and out to others.

Walk it out

- Spend some time reflecting on Paul's words in 2 Corinthians 12:7-10. What is the thorn in your flesh? The area of brokenness in your life? Have you experienced the healing power of Jesus' love to bind up this wound? If not, spend some time asking Jesus to do this for you.

- How do you respond to the idea that sharing our experience of God in the valleys of life is the ultimate act of hospitality? Have you ever experienced someone hosting you in this way?

- How could you host others through sharing your testimony of God working through your brokenness? Ask God for opportunities to do this.

Part 5

Signs of Spring

I believe that I shall see the goodness of the LORD

in the land of the living.

Psalm 27:13

Winter won't last forever

For now the winter is past,

the rain is over and gone.

The flowers appear on the earth.

Song of Solomon 2:11-12

We live very close to the Ridgeway, an ancient path that has been used for more than five thousand years. It runs for 87 miles from Avebury in Wiltshire to the Ivinghoe Beacon, north-west of London. I am fortunate to live near the stretch of this ancient path that passes the Uffington White Horse. I have the most wonderful group of fellow school mums whom I run with, and the Ridgeway is one of our favourite places to go. However, running there in the winter is hard work as the track is either a muddy bog or, after a hard frost, as slippery as an ice rink. On these runs, I find myself longing for spring and wondering whether the mud will ever go.

But the season does always change; spring comes and, with it, warmer, drier weather. Frosts become a thing of the past (for now), and the mud dries out. My friends and I find ourselves rewarded for all our hard work through winter as we get to run through some of the most beautiful countryside in the warmth of the spring sunshine while watching nature burst into life once again after the cold, dark winter. More than this, having experienced running in the depths of winter, we are especially grateful when spring comes. There is a deeper sense of joy having experienced the cold, the mud, the rain and the wind of winter.

Expanding the soul

The same is true in our lives too – while it might feel as though winter goes on forever, the season will change. Spring will come. God is always at work, restoring and redeeming, bringing new life to birth from what looked like death. As I have tried to articulate in all that has gone before, this new life might not look as we had hoped or expected it to look. We may not receive healing of the physical illness from which we so desperately want to be free. We might never have the family for which we long. Or we may never marry, or not marry again after a relationship breakdown. But there will always be new life. This is the new life of the Kingdom, a life that involves living more fully in our God-given identity and calling, and this is possible no matter what the circumstances of our lives.

Just like I appreciate running in spring much more having run through winter, I know that I appreciate the good things in life so much more now as a result of all that we walked through. As Jerry Sittser articulates so powerfully, 'sorrow ... enlarges the soul until the soul is capable of mourning and rejoicing simultaneously, of feeling the world's pain and hoping for its healing at the same time'.[179] I love how Sittser so perfectly describes the 'both–and' of the effects of sorrow. I know that walking through deep sorrow has given me a more tender heart. I find I can more readily empathise with and enter into the suffering of others. At the same time, I know I experience joy in a much deeper way too. When you have experienced the depths of grief, you don't take the joys of life for granted.

---

[179] Jerry Sittser, *A Grace Disguised*, p74.

The ruts of winter

However, although the mud of winter does dry out, the ruts from the mud of winter remain. The ground bears the marks of winter. Just as the ground I run on bears the ruts of winter, once you have walked through the pain of loss, your soul will always bear the marks of winter. I often say to people that, this side of death, there will always be a part of my soul in winter. One of the things that I got most angry about when Libby died was when people tried to comfort me by saying that I would 'get over it'. I realise that they were trying to help, but the truth is that I will never get over the loss of my daughter, nor of the other children I carried but never got to hold.

Sittser likens catastrophic loss to the amputation of a limb. While anyone who has lost an arm or a leg will, in time, learn to live without it, they will never forget they had it. 'Catastrophic loss by definition precludes recovery. It will transform or destroy us, but it will never leave us the same.'[180] This is what Libby's death has been like for me. I have learned to live without her, and with God's help I chose to be transformed rather than deformed by our losses. As a result, I have seen new life and beauty grow from the devastation.

I remember saying to friends not long after Libby had died that I would be happy if ultimately people reflected that Jon and I were never the same after her death. However, the change they saw in us had to be for the better. For me, this was about creating a positive legacy for my daughter. No parent wants their child associated with only loss and pain. When people think about Libby, I want them, like me, to be able to hold the tension of pain and heartache with hope, the hope that comes from having witnessed in our story the truth that God truly is present and at work no matter what we face in life. My prayer is that this hope will help them meet their own winter seasons with courage, authenticity, faith and hope.

---

[180] Jerry Sittser, *A Grace Disguised*, p73.

Restoration not replacement

When thinking about all of this, I am drawn to the end of the book of Job. Here we're told that God restored Job's fortunes and gave him twice as much as he had had before. Job had seven more sons and three more daughters and was wealthier than he had been before (Job 42:10-17). The temptation is to read this and think, well, that's good, God sorted all that out for Job. Yes, God did restore and, in true God style, what Job ended up with was more than what he had had before. But Job had still lost. He had witnessed the loss of all he had before: his livelihood, all the people who worked for him, his children, his health. Did the restoration we read about at the end of Job annul all these losses? The answer is no. No child that is born after the death of another child ever replaces the child who has died. Yes, they often bring an even more profound sense of joy than what would have been experienced before, but they can never cancel out the pain of the child who was lost. Added to this, walking through great suffering, as Job did, strips us of our naivety. We know that the worst things in life can and do happen and we are not exempt from them.

I talked in the previous chapter about how winter experiences are like wounds. The truth is that while we can turn to Jesus and ask Him to bind our wounds with His love, these wounds will never be fully healed in this life. Understanding this truth, that the death of my children was a deep wound I would live with for the rest of my life, led me to the big questions of what is the meaning of Christian hope, what and where is heaven, and what will happen when Jesus comes again?

On earth, as it is in heaven

I am the resurrection and the life. Those who believe in me,
even though they die, will live, and everyone who lives
and believes in me will never die.

John 11:25-26

Like many people who lose a loved one, when Libby died, my
thoughts turned to questions about heaven. For me, a crucial
part of Christian hope that I held on to with desperate
determination was that I had not lost my children forever; there
would come a day when we would be reunited, and I would get
to know them. As a result, this led me to think hard and read as
much as I could about heaven. Where is it? What is it like? Who
is there?

What I'm about to say might sound like a cop-out. But the
result of all my reading on heaven and what exactly the Christian
hope is, is that I'm not sure what heaven looks like for those
who die now.[181] To be honest, I'm OK with that because what
I do know is that heaven is where God lives and reigns, and it's

---

[181] If this is a subject that interests you, I found the following books
helpful: Paula Gooder, *Heaven* (SPCK, London, 2011); Tom Wright,
Surprised by Hope (SPCK, London, 2007); J Richard Middleton, *A New
Heaven and a New Earth: Reclaiming Biblical Eschatology* (Baker Academic,
Ada, 2014).

where Jesus went when He departed this world (Luke 24:51). This means that my children are with Jesus, and I can't think of a better person to entrust them to than Him. Crucially, though, I do know that heaven, as it exists now, is not the permanent dwelling place either of God or of those who have died.

Where is heaven?

I don't know about you, but I grew up with a very disembodied spiritual image of heaven, that it was somewhere our souls went when we died, and it would be one long worship service. Forever. More than this, when Jesus did come again, the earth would be destroyed, and we'd spend the rest of eternity as spirits in heaven. Call me a bad Christian, but heaven wasn't somewhere I really wanted to go, and certainly not a place where I wanted to live forever. I have to say I was somewhat relieved when, in all my reading about heaven after Libby died, I realised that this is not what the Bible teaches either about heaven or about what will happen when Jesus comes again.

Rather than being the place that we go to when we die, the Bible tells a very different story about heaven. Paula Gooder writes, 'Within the biblical tradition, the main portrayal of heaven is not as the final resting place for human beings or even as a place of contentment and bliss. Instead heaven is seen as the dwelling place of God.'[182] Biblically, heaven is the place where God dwells, and it is the place from which He reigns. Heaven is where God's will is perfectly carried out.

The Bible tells us that originally heaven and earth were not two separate entities.[183] God created a garden in which He placed Adam and Eve and in which He walked (Genesis 3:8).

---

[182] Paula Gooder, *Heaven*, p xiii.
[183] For a really great introduction to the concept of heaven and earth have a look at Bible Project's video on the topic, 'Heaven and Earth', https://bibleproject.com/explore/heaven-earth/ (accessed 23rd November 2020).

What's more, from the beginning, God's intention was missional. His plan was not that Adam and Eve should stay forever in the Garden of Eden. Humanity's original vocation was to work in partnership with God to rule and reign over God's good creation and extend the Garden of Eden and, thus, God's dwelling place throughout the earth.

Everything goes pear-shaped with the Fall, and we see heaven and earth separate. God's will is no longer perfectly enacted on earth and, as a result of sin, the earth is no longer God's dwelling place.

However, there are occasions and places where heaven and earth come together again, where heaven breaks in. The lines of communication have not been entirely cut. For example, in Genesis 28:10-17, we have the account of Jacob's dream of a stairway resting on the earth with its top reaching to heaven. The author of Genesis describes how angels were ascending and descending on this ladder. God then speaks to Jacob from the top of the ladder and promises him that He will give the land he is lying on to his descendants. When Jacob wakes up, he declares, 'Surely the LORD is in this place – and I did not know it! … How awesome is this place! This is none other than the house of God, and this is the gate of heaven.' Heaven and earth co-exist wherever God's presence is manifest.

This is why the Tabernacle and later the Temple were so important in the Old Testament. The Hebrew word *mishkan*, which we translate 'Tabernacle', means 'dwelling place'. The Tabernacle and then the Temple were the earthly dwelling places of God; as a result, they were the places where heaven and earth overlapped.

Moving into the New Testament, at the beginning of John's Gospel we're told that Jesus 'lived among us' (John 1:14). Literally, this means Jesus 'tabernacled' with us. What the apostle John is saying is that Jesus was a portable temple. He was the place where God dwelt. Wherever Jesus was, there heaven was too. Once again, we see heaven and earth overlapping, this time in the person of Jesus.

During His earthly ministry, Jesus preached that the Kingdom of God had come near; to use a technical term, He inaugurated the coming of the Kingdom. However, only when He comes again will heaven and earth be fully reunited. We live at the 'beginning of the end', if you like. Jesus initiated the inbreaking of heaven on earth, and when He comes again He will complete what He started.

In the last book of the Bible (Revelation), we see heaven and earth fully reunited in the new Jerusalem. Crucially, the apostle John tells us, the new Jerusalem doesn't have a Temple (Revelation 21:22). It doesn't need one because God's dwelling place will be with His people (Revelation 21:3). The 'union of heaven and earth is what the story of the Bible is all about'.[184]

We have a part to play in bringing about this union. As followers of Jesus, filled with the Holy Spirit, we are described by the Bible writers as the Temple of God (1 Corinthians 3:16; 6:19; 1 Peter 2:5). With the indwelling presence of the Holy Spirit, we now have the same ability as Jesus to reunite heaven and earth. What a picture this is, that all believers everywhere are 'mini temples' mediating the presence of God to those around them.

Crucially, though, we don't do this on our own. The apostles Paul and Peter are clear that it is as a community of believers filled with the Holy Spirit that we become a temple. We need each other. As the theologian Gregory Beale says, 'Our task as … the church is to be God's temple, so filled with his glorious presence that we expand and fill the earth with that presence until God finally accomplishes the goal completely at the end of time.'[185]

---

[184] Bible Project, 'Heaven and Earth'.
[185] G K Beale, *The Temple and the Church's Mission: A Biblical Theology of the Dwelling Place of God* (InterVarsity Press, Downers Grove, 2004), p402.

What is the Kingdom of God like?

The Bible tells us that heaven is where God reigns and where His will is perfectly enacted. But what does that look like? What would it look like to live in a world where heaven and earth overlap, where God dwells with His people and His will is done? Essentially, the question is, what is God's Kingdom like?

To answer this question, we can look at the life and ministry of Jesus. Jesus not only preaches that the Kingdom of God has come near, but He also demonstrates what the Kingdom looks like. Every time Jesus heals someone physically, releases the oppressed, feeds the hungry or raises the dead, we see the Kingdom in action. Essentially, Jesus restores broken, needy, fallen human beings. He reverses evil through releasing humans from every form of bondage, poverty and blindness. He reveals that God's will is for humanity to experience His *shalom* (completeness, safety, health, prosperity, peace) and His life-giving blessing.[186] Jesus also makes it clear that the restoration of God's *shalom* and blessing is not limited to humanity. Jesus teaches His disciples that when He comes again, all things will be renewed (Matthew 19:28).

Life in colour

As I have spoken about earlier, Libby's death led me to study the gospel message again, in particular, to look at the doctrine of salvation. What (or who) did Jesus save us from, and what does the salvation that Jesus offers look like?

I vividly remember being in a worship service one day when all these questions were swirling around in my head. In the middle of one song, a picture dropped into my mind. It was of a landscape, and at the forefront of this landscape was the cross. To begin with, the whole picture was in black and white, but as I watched, it was as though the black and white landscape was

---

[186] J Richard Middleton, *A New Heaven and a New Earth*, p260.

painted on a vast cloth that gradually got sucked into the centre of the cross. Underneath this black and white version of the picture was the real landscape in all its glorious colour.

This is the gospel message, that through His life, death and resurrection Jesus initiated not just the redemption of humanity but also the redemption of the whole world. As Tom Wright articulates:

> What has happened in the death and resurrection of Jesus Christ … is by no means limited to its effects on those human beings who believe the gospel and thereby find new life … It resonates out, in ways that we can't fully see or understand into the vast recesses of the universe.[187]

I love how Eugene Peterson unpacks this truth in *The Message*:

> He [Jesus] was supreme in the beginning and – leading the resurrection parade – he is supreme in the end. From beginning to end he's there, towering far above everything, everyone. So spacious is he, so roomy, that everything of God finds its proper place in him without crowding. Not only that, but all the broken and dislocated pieces of the universe – people and things, animals and atoms – get properly fixed and fit together in vibrant harmonies, all because of his death, his blood that poured down from the cross.
> *Colossians 1:18-20 (*The Message*)*

The salvation that God intends to bring about is holistic, encompassing the whole of the created order. God intends to restore and redeem the whole of His creation. God's plan is not to destroy the world but to redeem and restore it.

What's more, when God restores and redeems things, He doesn't simply take them back to what they were. As Walter

---

[187] Tom Wright, *Surprised by Hope*, p108.

Brueggemann writes, God's restoration is not 'a return to "the good old days"'.[188] When God restores, what we end up with is something more beautiful and more glorious than what we had before. When Jesus came back to life, it was not in a resuscitated body. No, He had a glorious resurrection body.[189] As the apostle Paul teaches us, Jesus' resurrection is the first fruits for those who believe (1 Corinthians 15:20). It is not a once-off occurrence but is what all believers in Him will experience. We will all be given glorious resurrection bodies.

This was a really powerful truth for me to hold on to when Libby died. She died because her body was not strong enough to endure labour. But the promise of God in Jesus is that her body that was buried in brokenness will be raised in glory. She was buried in weakness but will be raised in strength (1 Corinthians 15:43). This truth was so important to me that we had this verse engraved on Libby's headstone.

Think for a moment about all the brokenness – physical, emotional and spiritual – that we see in our lives and in the lives of those around us. All the corruption, abuse of power, injustice and oppression, and the misuse of the natural world. The Christian hope says that when Jesus comes again to establish the Kingdom fully, all of this will be redeemed and restored.

Seeing the Christian hope articulated in this way changes not just the way we think about the future. It changes the way we live now. It changes the way we treat our physical bodies, other people, our attitude to work, the natural world – basically, everything.

Who has access to the Kingdom?

The short answer to this question is, everyone. Let's turn for a moment to look at Jesus' teaching on this in the beatitudes

---

[188] Walter Brueggemann, *Virus as a Summons to Faith: Biblical Reflections in a Time of Loss, Grief, and Uncertainty* (Cascade Books, Salem, 2020), p30.
[189] Philippians 3:21.

(Matthew 5:3-10). Here, Jesus lists the groups of people who are blessed by God. The list includes the poor, those who mourn, the oppressed and the persecuted. For too long, we have misunderstood the meaning of Jesus' words here. We have thought that we have to make ourselves poor, or look for loss, or be subject to oppression or injustice in order to be blessed by God. But this is not what Jesus is saying. Jesus is coming against a first-century version of the prosperity gospel that says God blesses the righteous with wealth and a comfortable life. The point of Jesus' words is that being poor or having experienced loss or injustice or persecution doesn't annul our access to the Kingdom. It doesn't mean that God has retreated. No matter where we find ourselves in life, the message of the gospel is that God is with us through it all, and His Kingdom is available to everyone, no matter who they are or what the circumstances of their lives are.[190]

When will the Kingdom come?

The Bible teaches that the created world is waiting 'with eager longing for the revealing of the children of God' (Romans 8:19). Why is this important when it comes to the restoration of creation? To answer this, we need to go back to the beginning of the Bible and look at what the Genesis account says about human identity and calling (vocation).

The Genesis 1 account of the creation of humanity teaches that God made humans in His image and that He gave us delegated authority to rule over the created world and subdue it (Genesis 1:26-28). Being made in God's image, humanity was created to be the locus of the divine presence in the world.[191] Therefore, our original God-given calling was to be mediators of His presence on earth. We were to work in partnership with

---

[190] Dallas Willard, *The Divine Conspiracy: Rediscovering our Hidden Life in God* (William Collins, London, 2014), pp130-135.

[191] For more on this, see Richard Middleton, *The Liberating Image*.

Him to see the flourishing of His creation and the extension of His Kingdom. This is what it means to be human.

However, rather than partnering with God, we chose to go our own way. Instead of imaging God and using our power for the flourishing of the created world, we have abused our God-given authority. When combined with the mistaken belief that the physical world is ultimately going to be destroyed, this means that, rather than using our power in a creative, life-giving way to see the flourishing of creation, we have too often abused the physical world. We use both other humans and the natural world for what we can get out of them. We oppress other people and plunder natural resources for our own ends. Rather than seeing the flourishing of the created world, we live in a world where people are oppressed, and we fight wars over natural resources. As a result of the abuse of the natural world, we live in the middle of an environmental crisis. Our world does not experience the *shalom* and blessing that God intended.

Like the best of parents, God has not given up on humanity. He is determined to see our redemption; this is what the life, death and resurrection of Jesus are all about. Jesus inaugurated the renewal of all things, including humanity. Jesus showed us how to live a truly human life. He is our pattern. Rather than taking our power away, God in Jesus renews and redeems humanity. Humanity stepping back into their God-given identity and calling is what the natural world is waiting for. When this happens, we will see the extension of the Kingdom and the renewal and restoration of the created world. The biblical hope is of a redeemed and resurrected humanity ruling and reigning as we were originally intended to do, over a redeemed and restored creation.

Your Kingdom come

I realise this has been a whistle-stop tour of some huge concepts, but grasping these truths is fundamental to how we face our winter seasons. Instead of looking for a way out, we need to know that none of the awful things that happen to us separates us from the love of God or from life in His Kingdom. We need to know that death does not have the final word. Holding on to these truths is the way we will be able to walk through our winter seasons with hope and courage.

When Jesus comes again, He will complete the good work He started – the reunion of heaven and earth. One of my favourite verses in the Bible comes in Revelation 21, where we have the promise that when God's Kingdom is fully realised, and He comes to live with His people, 'Death will be no more; mourning and crying and pain will be no more, for the first things have passed away' (Revelation 21:4).

But we don't have to wait until Jesus comes again to see God's kingdom advance. In the prayer that He taught His disciples, Jesus calls us to pray for God's will to be done 'on earth as it is in heaven' (Matthew 6:10). Our call as His followers is to pray these same words and, through stepping back into our God-given identity and calling, to work to see God's Kingdom advance now.

As Dallas Willard articulated, the gospel is about more than forgiveness of sins and where we go when we die. It is an invitation to a new life in the Kingdom of God.[192] Spiritual formation is essentially the process of living in ever greater measure in God's Kingdom of *shalom* and blessing. Rather than living a fragmented life, God calls us to live a life where we experience His healing and *shalom* in every area of our lives. In physical, emotional and spiritual health. In our relationships with God, with our ourselves and with each other. And in our care for the created world. What's more, Jesus calls us to invite others into this life too. When we live this way, we experience the life-giving blessing of God.

God's people, His Church, are called to be an army of 'wounded warriors'. A people who, rather than allowing their hurt to hurt others, have invited Jesus to bind and transform

---

[192] Dallas Willard, *Renewing the Christian Mind*, p17.

their wounds, thus allowing their wounds to be a source of healing and transformation for others. A people whose lives and words bear witness to a God of love who longs to dwell with His people. A people who can weep with those who weep but also speak hope into the heartache. A people who can share the gospel message that no one and no situation, no matter how hard, is beyond the transforming, healing, redemptive love of God. A people who can proclaim that His Kingdom is for all people, everywhere. A people who know who they are and what God calls them to do. A people who know that they are beloved children of God, made in His image to manifest His presence on earth and called to partner with Him in the flourishing of His created world.

Through all the loss we walked through, I learnt how to live again. I learnt to live more fully in the Kingdom now and to look with hope and expectation to the renewal of all things. I also learnt how to love again, to love God and to love others more deeply. As a result, I am passionate to see the Kingdom come in greater measure in my life and in the lives of those I know and love.

My closing prayer for you is that, as you walk through your own winter season, you would learn to love again. You would know in a deep and intimate way the love of God, Father, Son, and Holy Spirit, holding you, strengthening you and sustaining you. And that you would learn to live again; that God's Kingdom of *shalom* and blessing would come in your life. May His streams of living water flow through you and from you to those you know and love.

Come, Lord Jesus.

Helpful websites if you have experienced the death of a baby or someone close to you

Miscarriage Association
https://www.miscarriageassociation.org.uk/

Stillbirth and Neonatal Death Society (Sands)
https://www.sands.org.uk/

Saying Goodbye
https://www.sayinggoodbye.org/

Cruse Bereavement Care
https://www.cruse.org.uk/

Care for the Family Bereavement Support
https://www.careforthefamily.org.uk/family-life/bereavement-support

For further reading

Suffering and loss

Gregory A Boyd, *Is God to Blame? Beyond Pat Answers to the Problem of Suffering* (InterVarsity Press, Downers Grove, 2003)

Pete Greig, *God on Mute: Engaging the Silence of Unanswered Prayer* (David C Cook, Lee Lance View, Colorado Springs, 2007)

Jerry Sittser, *A Grace Disguised: How the Soul Grows Through Loss*, expanded edition (Zondervan, Grand Rapids, 2004)

Who are You, God?

Bradley Jersak, *A More Christlike God: A More Beautiful Gospel* (Plain Truth Ministries, Pasadena, 2015)

Chris E W Green, *Surprised by God: How and Why What We Think about the Divine Matters* (Cascade Books, 2018)

Janet O Hagburg, *Who Are You, God? Suffering and Intimacy with God* (At River's Edge Press, Minneapolis, 2013)

Who am I?

David G Benner *Surrender to Love: Discovering the Heart of Christian Spirituality* (InterVarsity Press, Downers Grove,

2015). David Benner's book *The Gift of Being Yourself: The Sacred Call to Self Discovery* is also well worth reading.

J Richard Middleton, *The Liberating Image: The Imago Dei in Genesis 1* (Brazos Press, Grand Rapids, 2005). This is a more academic book but well worth the effort invested.

Henri J M Nouwen, *Life of the Beloved: Spiritual Living in a Secular World* (Crossroad Publishing Company, New York, 2002)

Mark Sayers, *The Vertical Self: How Biblical Faith Can Help Us Discover Who We Are in an Age of Self Obsession* (Thomas Nelson, Nashville, 2010)

Sheridan Voysey, *The Making of Us: Who We Can Become When Life Doesn't Go as Planned* (Thomas Nelson, Nashville, 2019)

Lament

Glenn Pemberton, *Hurting with God: Learning to Lament with the Psalms* (Abilene Christian University Press, Abilene, TX, 2012)

Hygge for the heartbroken

The following are my recommendations of books that will help you to understand why spiritual formation is important and how to create your own Rule of Life as you walk through winter.

David G Benner, *Opening to God: Lectio Divina and Life as Prayer* (InterVarsity Press, Downers Grove, 2010).

Brian Draper, *Soulfulness: Deepening the Mindful Life* (Hodder & Stoughton, London, 2016)

John Mark Comer, *The Ruthless Elimination of Hurry: How to Stay Emotionally Healthy and Spiritually Alive in the Chaos of the Modern World* (Hodder & Stoughton, London, 2019)

Justin Whitmel Earley, *The Common Rule: Habits of Purpose for an Age of Distraction* (InterVarsity Press, Downers Grove, 2019)

Richard Foster, *Streams of Living Water: Celebrating the Great Traditions of Christian Faith* (Hodder & Stoughton, London, 2017)

Abbot Christopher Jamison, *Finding Sanctuary: Monastic Steps for Everyday Life* (Orion Books Ltd, London, 2006)

M Robert Mulholland Jr, *Invitation to a Journey: A Road Map for Spiritual Formation*, expanded edition (InterVarsity Press, Downers Grove, 2016)

Lucy Peppiatt, *The Disciple: On Becoming Truly Human* (Cascade Books, Eugene, 2012)

Richard Rohr, *Falling Upward: A Spirituality for the Two Halves of Life* (SPCK, London, 2012)

Peter Scazzero, *Emotionally Healthy Spirituality: It's Impossible to Be Spiritually Mature While Remaining Emotionally Immature* (Zondervan, Grand Rapids, 2014)

Ann Voskamp, *One Thousand Gifts: A Dare to Live Fully Right Where You Are* (Zondervan, Grand Rapids, 2011)

Dallas Willard, *The Divine Conspiracy: Rediscovering our Hidden Life in God* (William Collins, London, 2014)

Opening ourselves to others

Brené Brown, *I Thought it Was Just Me (But It Isn't): Making the Journey from 'What Will People Think?' to 'I Am Enough'* (Avery, New York, 2008)

Brené Brown, *Daring Greatly: How the Courage to be Vulnerable Transforms the Way We Live, Love, Parent and Lead* (Penguin Life, London, 2012)

Henri J M Nouwen, *The Wounded Healer: In Our Own Woundedness We Can Become a Source of Life for Others* (Darton, Longman and Todd Ltd, London, 1994)

Heaven and Christian hope

J Richard Middleton, *A New Heaven and a New Earth: Reclaiming Biblical Eschatology* (Baker Academic, Ada, 2014)

Tom Wright, *Surprised by Hope* (SPCK, London, 2007)